Breakfasts & Brunches

GENERAL EDITOR
CHUCK WILLIAMS

RECIPES
NORMAN KOLPAS

PHOTOGRAPHY
ALLAN ROSENBERG

TIME
LIFE
BOOKS

TIME-LIFE BOOKS
Time-Life Books is a division of Time Life Inc.
Time-Life is a trademark of Time Warner Inc. U.S.A.

Time-Life Custom Publishing
Vice President and Publisher: Terry Newell
Managing Editor: Donia Ann Steele
Director of Acquisitions: Jennifer L. Pearce
Vice President of Sales and Marketing: Neil Levin
Director of Financial Operations: J. Brian Birky

WILLIAMS-SONOMA
Founder and Vice Chairman: Chuck Williams
Book Buyer: Victoria Kalish

WELDON OWEN INC.
President: John Owen
Vice President and Publisher: Wendely Harvey
Chief Operating Officer: Larry Partington
Vice President International Sales: Stuart Laurence
Managing Editor: Lisa Chaney Atwood
Consulting Editor: Norman Kolpas
Copy Editor: Sharon Silva
Design: John Bull, The Book Design Company
Production Director: Stephanie Sherman
Production Coordinator: Tarji Mickelson
Editorial Assistant: Sarah Lemas
Food Photographer: Allan Rosenberg
Additional Food Photography: Allen V. Lott
Food Stylist: Heidi Gintner
Prop Stylist: Sandra Griswold
Assistant Food Stylists: Nette Scott, Elizabeth C. Davis
Assistant Prop Stylist: Elizabeth C. Davis
Glossary Illustrations: Alice Harth

The Williams-Sonoma Kitchen Library
conceived and produced by Weldon Owen Inc.
814 Montgomery St., San Francisco, CA 94133

In collaboration with Williams-Sonoma
3250 Van Ness Ave., San Francisco, CA 94109

Printed in China by Toppan Printing Co., LTD.

A Note on Weights and Measures:
All recipes include customary U.S. and metric
measurements. Metric conversions are based on
a standard developed for these books and have
been rounded off. Actual weights may vary.

A Weldon Owen Production

Copyright © 1997 Weldon Owen Inc.
Reprinted in 1997, 1997; 1998; 1998
All rights reserved, including the right of
reproduction in whole or in part in any form.

Library of Congress
Cataloging-in-Publication Data:

Kolpas, Norman.
    Breakfasts & brunches / general editor, Chuck Williams ;
recipes, Norman Kolpas ; photography, Allan Rosenberg.
        p.   cm. — (Williams-Sonoma kitchen library)
    Includes index.
        ISBN 0-7835-0321-0
    1. Breakfasts.   2. Brunches.   I. Williams, Chuck.   II. Title.
III. Series.
TX733.K6522   1997
641.5'2—dc20   96-24077
                                                    CIP

Contents

Eggs & Dairy 15

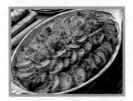

Brunch Main Dishes 35

Pancakes, Waffles, Breads & Cereals 53

Fruits & Vegetables 83

INTRODUCTION

"Breakfast like a king, dine like a pauper." That old adage sums up the wisdom of eating a satisfying, well-balanced morning meal—one that provides all the nutrients to start your day off right.

Nowadays, however, many people are too busy to eat a proper breakfast. Instead, as they hurry out the door, they grab a piece of toast or a muffin to go with their road mug of coffee. And then they wonder why they feel sluggish around midmorning.

This book aims to reverse that trend in several ways. First, it offers many breakfast recipes that take only minutes to prepare, and others that are easily made the night before. It also recognizes that a lot of us make up for busy weekdays by eating good breakfasts on weekends, or by entertaining with a leisurely late-morning Sunday brunch. A number of the recipes fulfill the broader range of menu items you're likely to serve on such occasions, among them uncomplicated dishes featuring meat, poultry or seafood.

On the following pages, you'll find information to help you assemble a wide array of morning dishes, including a survey of essential kitchen equipment; a guide to buying, storing and cooking eggs; and breakfast-making techniques and basic recipes. These fundamentals are followed by 45 delicious breakfast and brunch recipes.

Such variety returns us to the topic of eating a well-balanced morning meal. To that end, I encourage you to sample recipes from every chapter and then to compose for yourself, your family and friends some simple yet wholesome breakfast or brunch menus. After just a few easy, delicious morning meals, I know you'll begin to experience the benefits of breakfasting regularly.

Chuck Williams

EQUIPMENT

A broad array of equipment to serve every breakfast and brunch need, from omelets to coffee cakes, sausages to fruit compote

The same remarkable diversity that characterizes breakfast and brunch items is also found in the wide range of equipment shown here. Apart from such specialized pieces as an electric yogurt maker and an apple corer, virtually all of these kitchen tools and cookware perform multiple tasks that extend their usefulness far beyond morning cooking.

1. Stove-Top Grill Pan
Cast-iron pan with raised ridges reproduces the intense heat and the hatch marks of an outdoor grill. The channels between the ridges drain away fat, making the pan ideal for cooking bacon and sausages, as well as for grilling other meats, poultry and seafood.

2. Colander and Sieve
Durable stainless-steel colander and fine-mesh sieve for all-purpose draining of large and small items.

3. Kitchen Towel
Good-quality cotton towel for general kitchen cleanup.

4. Assorted Kitchen Tools
Crockery jar holds a slotted spoon for lifting poached eggs from simmering water; a wire whisk for stirring sauces, pancake and waffle batters, and for beating eggs; wooden spoons and spatula for all-purpose stirring; rubber spatula for blending batters and smoothing the surface of coffee cake batters before baking; and a ladle for serving cooked cereals and sauces.

5. Liquid Measuring Cup
For accurate measuring of liquid ingredients. Choose heat-resistant glass marked with fluid ounces and milliliters.

6. Gratin Dishes
Ovenproof porcelain or glazed earthenware dishes with shallow, sloping sides, designed to promote the formation of a golden crust—*gratin*, in French—during baking. May also be used for other baking or broiling needs, such as holding grapefruits or stuffed tomatoes.

7. Pot Holder
Heavy-duty cotton provides protection from hot cookware.

8. Instant-Read Thermometer
For accurately gauging the temperature of liquids when making homemade yogurt and sourdough starter.

9. Metal Spatula
Sturdy metal spatula with long, broad blade facilitates the turning of pancakes, hash browns, eggs and other breakfast items.

10. Zester
Small, sharp holes at end of stainless-steel blade cut citrus zest into fine shreds.

11. Apple Corer
For preparing apples for baking. Cylindrical blade with serrated edge cuts down vertically through an apple to easily remove its core.

12. Melon Baller
Sharp-edged, stainless-steel scoop cuts neat balls of melon and other soft fruits.

13. Chef's Knife
Large, all-purpose knife for chopping and slicing large items or large quantities of ingredients.

14. Paring Knife
For peeling vegetables, cutting up small ingredients and all-purpose trimming.

15. Grapefruit Knife
Small, curved, flexible blade with serrated edge loosens fruit segments from a grapefruit half while leaving them neatly in their shell.

16. Pastry Blender
For cutting butter or shortening into flour when making pastry or biscuit dough by hand.

17. Biscuit Cutter
Sturdy, circular metal cutter for forming biscuits from dough.

18. Rolling Pin
For rolling out quiche and tart pastry. Choose one with ball-bearing handles for smooth rolling, and a hardwood surface at least 12 inches (30 cm) long.

19. Sauté Pan
For poaching or scrambling eggs, cooking sausages or bacon and other general cooking uses.

20. Square Baking Pan
Standard 8-inch (20-cm) pan for baking coffee cakes. Choose good-quality heavy aluminum or tinplate steel.

21. Baking Sheet
For baking biscuits and toasting nuts and grains.

22. Tart Pan
Removable bottom of standard 9-inch (23-cm) pan allows tart to be unmolded. Fluted sides give crust an attractive edge.

23. Omelet Pan
Shallow pan with sloping sides, a long handle and, preferably, a nonstick surface, for easy cooking and folding of omelets.

24. Box Grater/Shredder
Stainless-steel tool for grating or shredding vegetables or cheeses by hand.

25. Mixing Bowls
Sturdy bowls in a range of sizes for mixing and serving.

26. Saucepan
For cooking hot breakfast cereals, compotes and sauces.

27. Yogurt Maker
Electric appliance maintains a steady incubation temperature for making yogurt at home. Six containers with lids transfer to the refrigerator for storage.

28. Measuring Spoons
For measuring small quantities of ingredients.

29. Dry Measuring Cups
For measuring dry ingredients, choose a sturdy metal set in graduated sizes, with straight rims for easy leveling.

30. Muffin Pan
For baking standard (½-cup/4-fl oz/125-ml) muffins.

Egg Basics

Cooked whole or scrambled, transformed into omelets or incorporated into batters or doughs for pancakes, waffles or sweet breads, eggs are the preeminent staple of the breakfast and brunch pantry.

Sizes and Grades

Eggs in the United States are sorted and sold in five sizes: small (approximately 1⅓ oz/40 g), medium (1½ oz/45 g), large (1¾ oz/50 g), extra large (2 oz/60 g) and jumbo (2¼ oz/67 g). The recipes in this book were developed with large eggs. Other sizes may be used in most egg dishes, although not for batters and doughs, which call for precise measurements to achieve the desired results.

Eggs are also graded AA, A or B, in descending order. These classifications take note of such factors as the quality and shape of the shell (shell color, however, is immaterial) and the thickness and clarity of the white. For recipes in which eggs will be beaten or blended, grade is insignificant; higher-grade eggs, however, will maintain more compact shapes when poached or fried because their whites are more viscous.

Freshness and Storage

The majority of eggs sold today reach markets within about a week of being laid. Considering that most eggs properly stored will keep in their shells for 4 to 5 weeks beyond the "sell by" date stamped on their cartons, keeping them fresh is seldom a problem. Refrigerate them in the carton, which both cushions them and guards against absorption of food odors. Do not leave eggs out on the kitchen counter: For every day left at room temperature, they will age the equivalent of more than a week in the refrigerator.

Poaching Eggs

For neatly poached eggs, use grade AA, the fresher the better. Adding a little vinegar to the poaching water helps the whites coagulate. Eggs may be poached up to 1 hour in advance and stored in a bowl of warm water; if needed, reheat in simmering water.

Slipping eggs into simmering water.
Half fill a large sauté pan with water and bring to a boil over high heat; reduce the heat to maintain a bare simmer. One at a time, break each egg into a small cup or saucer. Holding the cup or saucer near the water, gently slip the egg into it.

Cooking and trimming the poached eggs.
Continue poaching, basting once or twice with the simmering water, until the whites are completely set and the yolks look glazed but are still soft, 3½–4 minutes. Using a slotted spoon, lift each egg out of the water and use a knife to trim the ragged edges.

SCRAMBLING EGGS

The key to successful scrambled eggs lies in slow, gentle cooking and constant stirring, resulting in creamy curds. While you have some leeway in cooking the eggs softer or firmer to your taste, take care to avoid overcooking them to the point of being dry or rubbery.

Lightly beating the eggs.
Break the eggs into a mixing bowl. Using a wire whisk or a fork, beat the eggs vigorously but briefly, just until the yolks and whites are blended and only slightly frothy.

Stirring and scraping.
Melt butter in a regular or nonstick frying pan over medium-low heat. Add the beaten eggs and cook, slowly stirring and scraping with a wooden spatula as the eggs form curds. Continue until the eggs are done to your liking but are still soft, moist and creamy.

MAKING OMELETS

Think of an omelet as scrambled eggs cooked pancake style and then folded, usually around a filling. Cooking the eggs slowly over low heat yields tender results. The technique of simultaneously sliding the omelet from the pan and folding it in half is easily mastered.

Cooking the eggs.
Melt butter in an omelet pan over medium heat. Add the lightly beaten, seasoned eggs. As the eggs begin to set along the edges, use a fork or spatula to push the edges toward the center, tilting the pan to let the liquid egg on top flow to the edges and run underneath.

Folding the omelet.
When the eggs are almost set but still slightly moist on top, spoon any prepared filling over half of the surface. Shake the pan to loosen the omelet. Lift and tilt the pan to slide out the omelet, filled side first, onto a plate; when it is halfway out, tip the pan over the plate to fold the omelet.

Breakfast & Brunch Techniques

Breakfast and brunch may be the simplest meals to make. But mastering a few techniques, along with the basic recipes on the following pages, will help you prepare morning dishes with even greater ease.

Preparing Citrus Fruits

Because their segments are encased in tough membranes, citrus fruits require advance preparation to make them more attractive to serve and pleasurable to eat.

Preparing grapefruit.
Cut the grapefruit in half. Using a curved, serrated grapefruit knife in a sawing motion, loosen the fruit segments for easier eating by cutting around the perimeter between the fruit and the white pith; then cut around each segment to separate it from the surrounding membrane.

Cutting citrus segments.
Cut a thick slice off both ends of the citrus fruit. Stand the fruit upright and, following its contours, slice off the peel, pith and membrane in thick strips. Holding the fruit over a bowl, cut along each side of the membrane to free each segment, letting it drop into the bowl.

Making Pancakes

Whether called pancakes, flapjacks, hoecakes or other names, these rounds of griddle-cooked batter will be at their most tender if the batter is mixed lightly, so that the flour's gluten does not overdevelop. Keep a watchful eye for the right moment to flip the pancakes.

Flipping pancakes.
Pour prepared batter onto a lightly greased, hot frying pan or griddle to form individual pancakes. When their edges appear dry and their surface is covered with bubbles, slip a spatula underneath to flip them.

Cooking Hash

Taking its name from the French *hacher,* "to chop," hash combines meat, poultry or seafood with potatoes, other vegetables and milk or cream to bind. Cooked as a large cake, the loosely bound mixture calls for careful turning.

Flipping a hash cake.
Pack the hash into a greased nonstick frying pan and cook until its underside is crisp and golden. Using a spatula, loosen the edges and invert a flat heatproof plate on top; carefully flip them together. Lift away the pan. Then, slide the cake back into the pan to brown the other side.

Sourdough Starter

Although many markets, health-food stores and cookware shops sell packets of dried sourdough starter, you can make your own by following these simple directions. You will need to begin making the starter 2–3 days in advance of using it. If your starter mixture does not look bubbly within 24 hours, discard it and start again.

1 tablespoon active dry yeast
1 cup (8 fl oz/250 ml) lukewarm water (110°F/43°C)
1 cup (5 oz/155 g) all-purpose (plain) flour
1 tablespoon sugar

*I*n a bowl, dissolve the yeast in the lukewarm water. Stir in the flour and sugar. Cover partially and let stand at warm room temperature until the mixture begins to bubble and smell sour, 2–3 days.

The starter is now ready to use. Measure out the amount you need, then replenish the starter by stirring in ½ cup (2½ oz/75 g) flour and ½ cup (4 fl oz/125 ml) lukewarm water. Cover the starter loosely and store in the refrigerator indefinitely, replenishing it as directed each time some is removed.

Makes about 1½ cups (12 fl oz/375 ml)

Citrus Segments in
Vanilla Bean Syrup

Sourdough
Starter

Sourdough Pancakes
with Blueberries

Homemade Yogurt

The active cultures in homemade yogurt provide a wonderful tangy flavor and aid in digestion. The easiest, most foolproof way to make yogurt at home is to buy an inexpensive yogurt maker, sold in some kitchen-supply and health-food stores. Start making the yogurt at least one night before you plan to serve it. For flavored yogurt, stir in chopped fresh fruit, vanilla or other flavor extracts (essences), jelly or jam, or puréed berries or other soft fruits; sweeten to taste with sugar or honey.

4 cups (32 fl oz/1 l) whole or low-fat milk
½ cup (4 oz/125 g) nonpasteurized whole-milk or
   low-fat plain yogurt containing active yogurt
   cultures, at room temperature

*P*our the milk into a saucepan; place over medium heat. Bring to a boil and immediately remove from the heat.

   Place the end of an instant-read thermometer in the pan of milk. When the milk has cooled to lukewarm (110°F/43°C), combine about 1 cup (8 fl oz/250 ml) of the milk and the yogurt in a bowl. Stir until smooth; then, stirring constantly, slowly pour the mixture back into the pan of warm milk.

   Pour the milk-yogurt mixture into the containers of a home yogurt maker and process overnight according to the manufacturer's directions. Serve warm the next morning, or cover and refrigerate before serving. Store, tightly covered, in the refrigerator for up to 1 week. Reserve some of the homemade yogurt to begin making your next batch, if you like.

Makes about 4 cups (2 lb/1 kg)

Basic Quiche and Tart Pastry

Use this easy recipe to make the pastry shells for brunch quiches (pages 16 and 23) and for the fresh fruit tart on page 86.

1½ cups (7½ oz/235 g) all-purpose (plain) flour
½ teaspoon salt
¼ cup (2 oz/60 g) unsalted butter, chilled
¼ cup (2 oz/60 g) vegetable shortening
3–4 tablespoons cold water

*I*n a mixing bowl, stir together the flour and salt. Add the butter and shortening and, using a pastry blender or 2 knives, cut them in until the mixture resembles coarse bread crumbs. Sprinkle in the water, 1 tablespoon at a time, stirring gently with a fork after each addition and adding only enough of the water to form a rough mass.

   Using floured hands, pat the dough into a smooth, round flattened disk. Use immediately, or wrap in plastic wrap and refrigerate for up to 2 days.

Makes enough dough for one 9-inch (23-cm) quiche or tart shell

Homemade Yogurt

Fresh Fruit and Lemon Curd Tart

Homemade Yogurt with Fresh and Puréed Berries

Citrus Hollandaise

Orange and lemon juices and zests provide a pleasantly sharp contrast to the richness of classic hollandaise sauce.

1 cup (8 oz/250 g) unsalted butter, cut into pieces
4 egg yolks
1 teaspoon grated orange zest
1 teaspoon grated lemon zest
2 teaspoons fresh orange juice
2 teaspoons fresh lemon juice
½ teaspoon salt
¼ teaspoon dry mustard

*I*n a small saucepan over low heat, melt the butter. Remove from the heat.

Put the egg yolks, orange and lemon zests and juices, salt and mustard in a blender or in a food processor fitted with the metal blade. Process until smooth. With the motor running, slowly drizzle in the butter. The sauce will gradually emulsify to a thick, smooth, creamy consistency.

Once the butter is incorporated and the correct consistency is achieved, stop the machine and transfer the sauce to a small metal or glass bowl. Set the bowl over (not touching) hot water in a larger bowl or pan to keep the sauce warm. Cover and keep warm until ready to use, up to about 30 minutes.

Makes about 1½ cups (12 fl oz/375 ml)

Quick Tomato Sauce

In a matter of minutes, you can prepare this flavorful sauce to complement all sorts of savory breakfast or brunch dishes. Plum (Roma) tomatoes are your best bet for year-round flavor. If you like, peel the tomatoes before seeding and chopping them.

2 tablespoons olive oil
2 cloves garlic, finely chopped
1 lb (500 g) plum (Roma) tomatoes, seeded and
    coarsely chopped
1 teaspoon sugar
2 tablespoons finely sliced fresh basil leaves
1 tablespoon finely chopped fresh flat-leaf (Italian)
    parsley
salt and freshly ground pepper

*I*n a frying pan over medium-high heat, warm the olive oil. Add the garlic and, when it sizzles, stir in the tomatoes and sugar. Sauté, stirring, just until the tomatoes' juices begin to thicken, 5–7 minutes.

Stir in the basil and parsley and season to taste with salt and pepper.

Makes about 1½ cups (12 fl oz/375 ml)

Citrus Hollandaise

Quick Tomato Sauce

Poached Eggs Neptune

1 tablespoon distilled white or cider
    vinegar
1 teaspoon salt
8 eggs
2 tablespoons unsalted butter
1 lb (500 g) cooked bay shrimp
1 tablespoon finely chopped fresh dill
    or 1½ teaspoons dried dill
4 English muffins or 8 crumpets
citrus hollandaise *(recipe on page 13)*,
    warm
8 small fresh dill sprigs or 1 teaspoon
    finely chopped fresh chives

A refreshing change of pace from classic eggs Benedict, this recipe features the tiny precooked shrimp, commonly called bay shrimp, sold in the fresh seafood sections of most food stores. Choose very fresh eggs for the best results.

*I*n a large sauté pan, pour in water to a depth of 2 inches (5 cm) and bring to a boil. Add the vinegar and salt and reduce the heat to a gentle simmer; there should be only a few bubbles breaking on the surface of the water. Break 1 egg into a small cup or saucer, taking care not to break the yolk. Then, holding the cup or saucer near the surface of the water, gently slide in the egg. Repeat with the other eggs; add only as many as will fit comfortably in the pan. Cook until the whites are firm and the yolks look slightly opaque, 3½–4 minutes. Using a slotted spoon, lift out each egg and, using a small knife, trim off any ragged edges. Transfer to a bowl of warm water to keep warm until ready to serve.

In a small frying pan over low heat, melt the butter. Add the shrimp and dill and sauté, stirring, until warmed through, about 1 minute.

Meanwhile, split and toast the muffins (or toast the crumpets). Place 2 muffin halves (or 2 crumpets), split sides up, on each warmed individual plate. Top each with an equal amount of the shrimp. Using the slotted spoon, transfer each egg to a folded kitchen towel to drain briefly, then place atop the shrimp. Spoon the warm hollandaise evenly over each egg and garnish with the dill sprigs or chives. Serve at once.

Serves 4

Leek and Canadian Bacon Quiche

basic quiche and tart pastry (recipe on
  page 12)
6 slices Canadian bacon, cut into strips
  1 inch (2.5 cm) long by ¼ inch (6 mm)
  wide
1 tablespoon unsalted butter
1 leek, including tender green tops,
  carefully washed and cut crosswise
  into slices ¼ inch (6 mm) thick
3 eggs
1½ cups (12 fl oz/375 ml) half-and-half
  (half cream)
¼ teaspoon salt
¼ teaspoon freshly ground pepper
6 oz (185 g) Gruyère or Jarlsberg cheese,
  shredded
1½ teaspoons cornstarch (cornflour)

This savory tart is an adaptation of the classic quiche Lorraine.

Preheat an oven to 425°F (220°C).

On a lightly floured work surface, roll out the pastry dough into a round 12 inches (30 cm) in diameter. Drape the round over the rolling pin and carefully transfer to a 9-inch (23-cm) tart pan with a removable bottom. Gently ease the pastry into the pan. Trim the pastry even with the pan rim.

Prick the bottom and sides of the pastry shell with fork tines. Form a double-thick 12-inch (30-cm) square of aluminum foil, poke a few holes in it, then press it into the pastry-lined pan. Bake for 8 minutes. Remove the foil and bake until the pastry looks dry but not brown, about 4 minutes longer. Remove from the oven; reduce the temperature to 325°F (165°C).

In a nonstick frying pan over medium heat, sauté the bacon until it begins to brown, 2–3 minutes. Using a slotted spoon, transfer to paper towels to drain. Pour off the fat and add the butter to the pan. Melt over medium-low heat and add the leek. Sauté, stirring frequently, until tender, about 10 minutes. Set aside.

In a bowl, using a fork, beat the eggs until lightly frothy. Stir in the half-and-half, salt and pepper. In another bowl, toss the cheese with the cornstarch. Add the cheese, bacon and leek to the egg mixture and stir well. Pour into the pastry shell.

Bake until a knife inserted into the center comes out clean, 35–40 minutes. If the edges are browning too quickly, cover them with strips of aluminum foil.

Transfer to a rack to cool for 15 minutes. Remove the pan rim and place the quiche on a serving plate. Serve warm.

Makes one 9-inch (23-cm) quiche; serves 4–6

Classic Fines Herbes Omelet

3 eggs
¼ teaspoon salt
pinch of ground white pepper
1 tablespoon unsalted butter
1 teaspoon finely chopped fresh flat-leaf
    (Italian) parsley
1 teaspoon finely chopped fresh chives
1 teaspoon finely chopped fresh chervil
½ teaspoon finely chopped fresh tarragon

This definitive French omelet features a classic combination of herbs: parsley, chervil, chives and tarragon. Feel free to use any or all of them, as your taste dictates. The recipe yields 1 serving, as omelets are best made individually.

*I*n a bowl, using a fork or wire whisk, beat together the eggs, salt and white pepper until lightly frothy.

In an 8-inch (20-cm) nonstick omelet pan over medium heat, melt the butter. Add the eggs and, as they begin to set, using a fork or spatula, carefully lift the edges and gently push them toward the center, tilting the pan slightly to allow the liquid egg on top to flow underneath. Continue to cook until the eggs are almost completely set but still slightly moist on top, 3–4 minutes.

Evenly sprinkle the parsley, chives, chervil and tarragon over the surface of the eggs. Shake the pan; if the omelet does not slip easily, carefully loosen the edges with the fork or spatula. Carefully slide the omelet from the pan to a warmed plate and, when halfway out, quickly flip the pan over to fold the omelet in half. Serve at once.

Serves 1

Scrambled Eggs with Lox and Sweet Onions

2 tablespoons unsalted butter

½ sweet yellow onion such as Vidalia, Walla Walla or Maui, finely chopped

12 eggs, lightly beaten

6 oz (185 g) thinly sliced lox (see note), cut into strips 1 inch (2.5 cm) long and ¼ inch (6 mm) wide

freshly ground pepper

1 tablespoon finely chopped fresh chives

A favorite delicatessen dish gets extra refinement from sweet onion. If the slightly oily smoked salmon known as lox is unavailable, use any cold-smoked salmon. Serve with split and toasted bagels.

*I*n a frying pan over medium-low heat, melt the butter. Add the onion and sauté, stirring, until it just begins to turn golden, 3–5 minutes.

Add the eggs, raise the heat slightly and stir and scrape as soft curds begin to form. While the eggs are still fairly liquid, scatter in the lox, season to taste with pepper and continue stirring and scraping until cooked to the desired doneness.

Transfer to warmed individual plates and garnish with the chives. Serve at once.

Serves 4–6

Broccoli and Goat Cheese Quiche

basic quiche and tart pastry *(recipe on page 12)*
1 cup (2 oz/60 g) small broccoli florets
3 eggs
2 green (spring) onions, including some tender green tops, thinly sliced
1½ cups (12 fl oz/375 ml) milk
¼ teaspoon salt
¼ teaspoon freshly ground pepper
⅛ teaspoon freshly grated nutmeg
6 oz (185 g) creamy fresh goat cheese

Two strong-flavored ingredients in their own right, broccoli and goat cheese become pleasantly tamer when combined in this quiche.

*P*reheat an oven to 425°F (220°C).

On a lightly floured work surface, roll out the pastry dough into a round 12 inches (30 cm) in diameter. Drape the round over the rolling pin and carefully transfer to a 9-inch (23-cm) tart pan with removable bottom. Gently ease the pastry into the pan. Trim the pastry even with the pan rim.

Prick the bottom and sides of the pastry shell with fork tines. Form a double-thick 12-inch (30-cm) square of aluminum foil, poke a few holes in it, then press it into the pastry-lined pan. Bake for 8 minutes. Remove the foil and bake until the pastry looks dry but not brown, about 4 minutes longer. Remove from the oven; reduce the temperature to 325°F (165°C).

Bring a saucepan three-fourths full of lightly salted water to a boil. Add the broccoli and cook until tender-crisp, about 5 minutes. Drain well, pat dry and set aside. In a bowl, using a fork, beat the eggs until lightly frothy. Stir in the green onions, milk, salt, pepper and nutmeg.

Scatter the broccoli evenly in the pastry shell. Drop small clumps of the goat cheese evenly among the florets; carefully pour in the egg mixture. Bake until a knife inserted into the center comes out clean, 35–40 minutes. If the edges are browning too quickly, cover them with strips of aluminum foil.

Transfer to a rack to cool for 15 minutes. Remove the pan rim and place the quiche on a serving plate. Serve warm.

Makes one 9-inch (23-cm) quiche; serves 4–6

Sweet Omelet Soufflé with Caramelized Bananas

6 tablespoons (3 oz/90 g) unsalted butter
2 firm but ripe bananas, peeled and cut
  crosswise into slices ¼ inch (6 mm)
  thick
¼ cup (2 oz/60 g) granulated sugar
6 eggs, separated
2 tablespoons confectioners' (icing) sugar
pinch of salt

Serve this elegant omelet as the centerpiece of a special breakfast or brunch for two.

*I*n a small frying pan over medium heat, melt 3 tablespoons of the butter. Add the banana slices and, using a fork, turn to coat them well with butter. Sauté until very lightly browned, 2–3 minutes.

Sprinkle the bananas evenly with the granulated sugar. Reduce the heat slightly and continue to sauté until the sugar melts, turns a light caramel color and coats the bananas, 3–5 minutes. Remove from the heat, cover to keep warm and set aside.

Put the egg whites in a bowl. Add the confectioners' sugar and salt and beat with a wire whisk just until very frothy but still fairly liquid. In another bowl, beat the yolks until blended. Using the whisk, gradually stir the whites into the yolks until fully incorporated.

In an 8-inch (20-cm) nonstick omelet pan over medium heat, melt the remaining 3 tablespoons butter. Add the eggs and, as they begin to set, using a fork or spatula, carefully lift the edges and gently push them toward the center, tilting the pan slightly to allow the liquid egg on top to flow underneath. Continue to cook until the eggs are almost completely set but still slightly moist on top, 4–5 minutes.

Arrange the bananas evenly over half of the omelet. Shake the pan; if the omelet does not slip easily, carefully loosen the edges with the fork or spatula. Beginning with the banana-covered side of the omelet, slide the omelet from the pan to a warmed serving plate and, when halfway out, flip the pan over to fold the omelet in half over the bananas. Cut in half and serve at once.

Serves 2

Denver Scramble

2 tablespoons unsalted butter

½ yellow onion, cut into ½-inch (12-mm) dice

½ green bell pepper (capsicum), seeded, deribbed and cut into ½-inch (12-mm) squares

½ red bell pepper (capsicum), seeded, deribbed and cut into ½-inch (12-mm) squares

6 oz (185 g) smoked ham or Canadian bacon, cut into ½-inch (12-mm) dice

8 eggs, lightly beaten

salt and ground white pepper

2 oz (60 g) Cheddar cheese, shredded (optional)

1 tablespoon finely chopped fresh flat-leaf (Italian) parsley

This Western diner-style recipe may be better known as an omelet, but the casual nature of its embellishments are well suited to a scramble—in essence, an omelet in which the filling is mixed with the eggs. If you like, accompany with quick tomato sauce (recipe on page 13).

In a nonstick frying pan over medium-low heat, melt the butter. Add the onion and green and red bell peppers and sauté, stirring frequently, until the vegetables are tender-crisp, 2–3 minutes. Add the ham or Canadian bacon and sauté for 1 minute longer.

Add the eggs to the pan, season to taste with salt and white pepper and cook over medium-low heat, stirring and scraping frequently, until the eggs form soft, moist curds that bind the other ingredients, 2–3 minutes. Stir in the Cheddar cheese, if using, and continue stirring and scraping until the eggs are done to your liking.

Spoon onto warmed individual plates and garnish with the parsley. Serve at once.

Serves 4

Corn-and-Egg Pudding with Ham and Cheese

2 whole eggs, plus 2 egg yolks

2½ cups (15 oz/470 g) fresh corn kernels (from 8–10 ears)

½ cup (4 fl oz/125 ml) heavy (double) cream

¼ lb (125 g) smoked ham, finely chopped

¼ lb (125 g) Gruyère or Jarlsberg cheese, shredded

½ teaspoon sweet paprika

This recipe takes its inspiration from a favorite creation of legendary New York Times *food writer Craig Claiborne. His version uses Cheddar cheese and a zesty dose of diced green chilies. You may substitute 2½ cups (1¼ lb/625 g) canned creamed corn (preferably the kind without added starch) for the fresh corn.*

Preheat an oven to 375°F (190°C). Butter a 1½-qt (1.5-l) shallow baking dish.

In a bowl, using a fork, lightly beat together the whole eggs and egg yolks until blended. Briskly stir in the corn and cream until well combined. Stir in the ham, cheese and paprika.

Pour the corn mixture into the prepared dish. Bake until puffy and lightly golden, 25–35 minutes. Scoop onto warmed individual plates and serve at once.

Serves 4–6

Crab Meat and Bay Shrimp Omelet

3 eggs
¼ teaspoon salt
pinch of ground white pepper
1½ tablespoons unsalted butter
1 oz (30 g) cooked bay shrimp
1 oz (30 g) flaked cooked crab meat
¼ teaspoon grated lemon zest
fresh dill sprigs or flat-leaf (Italian)
   parsley or chervil leaves

Precooked crab meat and small shrimp from the fish market make an ideal and easy omelet filling. Warming the filling gently with a dab of butter ensures that it will be hot when folded inside. For a more indulgent dish, top with citrus hollandaise (recipe on page 13), or omit the lemon zest and serve the omelets with quick tomato sauce (page 13).

*I*n a bowl, using a fork or wire whisk, beat the eggs together with the salt and white pepper until lightly frothy.

In a small frying pan or saucepan over low heat, melt ½ tablespoon of the butter. Add the bay shrimp and crab meat and sauté until just heated through, 1–2 minutes. Stir in the lemon zest, cover to keep warm and set aside.

In an 8-inch (20-cm) nonstick omelet pan over medium heat, melt the remaining 1 tablespoon butter. Add the eggs. As they begin to set, using a fork or spatula, carefully lift the edges and gently push them toward the center, tilting the pan slightly to allow the liquid egg on top to flow underneath. Continue to cook until the eggs are almost completely set but still slightly moist on top, 3–4 minutes.

Evenly sprinkle the shrimp and crab mixture over half of the omelet. Shake the pan; if the omelet does not slip easily, carefully loosen the edges with the fork or spatula. Beginning with the shellfish-covered side of the omelet, carefully slide the omelet from the pan to a warmed plate and, when halfway out, flip the pan over to fold the omelet in half over the filling. Garnish with dill, parsley or chervil and serve at once.

Serves 1

Zucchini Frittata

1½ lb (750 g) small zucchini (courgettes), trimmed and cut crosswise into very thin slices
salt
10 eggs
¼ cup (1 oz/30 g) freshly grated Parmesan cheese
freshly ground pepper
2 tablespoons unsalted butter
2 tablespoons olive oil
quick tomato sauce (*recipe on page 13*), warmed

Frittata is the term for a type of rustic Italian flat omelet. Slice the zucchini thinly for the best texture. Salting the slices helps to draw out excess moisture before they are combined with the eggs.

*E*venly spread one-third of the zucchini slices in a colander set over a bowl. Sprinkle with salt. Spread half of the remaining slices over the first layer of zucchini, salt them, then spread and salt the remainder. Set aside to drain for 30 minutes. Then, pick up the zucchini in small handfuls and squeeze out the juices. Set aside.

Preheat an oven to 350°F (180°C).

In a bowl, using a fork, beat the eggs until lightly frothy. Add the zucchini and half of the cheese and stir gently to combine; season to taste with pepper.

In a 10-inch (25-cm) ovenproof, nonstick frying pan over medium heat, melt the butter with the olive oil. Add the zucchini-egg mixture, spreading it evenly. Sprinkle with the remaining cheese. Place in the oven and bake until set but still slightly moist, about 20 minutes.

Serve the frittata directly from the pan, or loosen the edges with a knife tip and slide it out or invert it onto a warmed platter. Cut into wedges and top with the tomato sauce. Serve at once.

Serves 4–6

Ham-and-Potato Gratin

2 lb (1 kg) Yukon Gold or other waxy
　　yellow potatoes, unpeeled
¾ cup (3 oz/90 g) freshly grated
　　Parmesan cheese
3 oz (90 g) thinly sliced smoked ham,
　　torn into bite-sized pieces
salt and ground white pepper
1 tablespoon cornstarch (cornflour)
1 cup (8 fl oz/250 ml) low-fat milk
2 teaspoons Dijon-style mustard
3–5 drops hot-pepper sauce, optional
1 tablespoon unsalted butter
2 tablespoons chopped fresh flat-leaf
　　(Italian) parsley

The results of this simple assembly are tender, incredibly rich-tasting potatoes imbued with the smoky taste of good-quality ham. You could also make it with smoked turkey. Serve the gratin alongside your favorite eggs, or as a satisfying brunch dish on its own. Or make the dish without meat and serve it with a brunch ham.

Preheat an oven to 375°F (190°C). Butter a 12-inch (30-cm) oval gratin dish.

Cut the potatoes crosswise into slices no more than ¼ inch (6 mm) thick. Place half of the potatoes in a layer on the bottom of the prepared dish, arranging them in overlapping concentric circles like roof shingles. Sprinkle with about one-third of the cheese and arrange the ham on top. Layer the remaining potatoes on top, overlapping them as before. Season to taste with salt and white pepper, then sprinkle evenly with the remaining cheese.

Add the cornstarch to the cup in which you have measured the milk and stir until dissolved. Then stir in the mustard until thoroughly blended. Add the hot-pepper sauce, if using. Pour the mixture evenly over the potatoes. Cut the butter into bits and dot it over the top.

Bake until the potatoes are tender when pierced with the tip of a sharp knife and the top is deep golden brown, about 1 hour. Spoon onto warmed serving plates, sprinkle with the parsley and serve hot.

Serves 4–6

Corned Beef Hash

1¼ lb (625 g) Yukon Gold or other
  waxy yellow potatoes, unpeeled, cut
  into ½-inch (12-mm) dice
2 tablespoons unsalted butter
1 large mild yellow onion, cut into
  ½-inch (12-mm) dice
1 green or red bell pepper (capsicum),
  seeded, deribbed and cut into ½-inch
  (12-mm) squares
1½ lb (750 g) unsliced cooked lean
  corned beef, cut into ½-inch (12-mm)
  dice
⅓ cup (3 fl oz/80 ml) milk
½ cup (¾ oz/20 g) finely chopped fresh
  parsley, plus parsley sprigs for garnish
2 tablespoons finely chopped fresh
  chives
salt and freshly ground pepper
4 tablespoons (2 fl oz/60 ml) vegetable oil

This diner favorite can also be made with leftover roast beef, ham or cooked chicken. Serve individual portions topped with poached eggs (directions on page 8), or pass quick tomato sauce (recipe on page 13).

Place the potatoes in a saucepan with lightly salted cold water to cover. Bring to a boil over high heat; reduce the heat to medium and simmer, uncovered, until just tender enough to pierce with a fork, 5–7 minutes.

Meanwhile, in a nonstick frying pan over medium heat, melt the butter. Add the onion and bell pepper and sauté until the onion is tender-crisp, 4–5 minutes. Set aside.

Drain the potatoes and place in a bowl. Add the onion and bell pepper; set the frying pan aside and do not wash it. Add to the bowl the corned beef, milk, chopped parsley and chives. Toss to mix well, taking care not to mash the potato pieces; season to taste with salt and ground pepper and toss again.

Heat 2 tablespoons of the oil in the reserved frying pan over medium heat. Add the hash mixture, pressing it down with the back of a spatula to form an even, compact cake. Reduce the heat to medium-low and cook, shaking the pan occasionally, until crusty and lightly browned on the bottom, about 15 minutes. If the hash cake does not move freely, use the spatula to loosen the edges. Invert a large heatproof plate over the pan. Using oven mitts, firmly hold the pan and plate together and invert them. Lift off the pan.

Heat the remaining 2 tablespoons oil in the same pan and slide the hash cake, browned side up, back into it, tucking any stray pieces back into place. Cook until the second side is crusty, about 10 minutes longer. Unmold onto the same plate and cut into wedges. Garnish with parsley sprigs and serve hot.

Serves 4

Tournedos of Poached Salmon on Lemon Rice

FOR THE LEMON RICE:
1½ cups (12 fl oz/375 ml) water
½ teaspoon salt
1 tablespoon unsalted butter
1 cup (7 oz/220 g) long-grain white rice
1 tablespoon grated lemon zest
1 tablespoon finely chopped fresh dill
1 tablespoon finely chopped fresh chives

FOR THE SALMON AND THE SAUCE:
2 cups (16 fl oz/500 ml) dry white wine
2 cups (16 fl oz/500 ml) fish stock
   or bottled clam juice
1 yellow onion, thinly sliced
1 carrot, thickly sliced
1 celery stalk, cut into chunks
2 large fresh flat-leaf (Italian) parsley
   sprigs
2 bay leaves
½ teaspoon whole white peppercorns
1 lb (500 g) center-cut salmon fillet,
   skinned
salt and ground white pepper
4 yellow bell peppers (capsicums),
   seeded, deribbed, roasted and peeled
   (see glossary, page 104)
2 tablespoons olive oil

fresh flat-leaf (Italian) parsley or
   dill sprigs

*T*o make the lemon rice, bring the water and salt to a boil in a saucepan. Add the butter and stir in the rice. Reduce the heat to very low, cover and cook until the rice is tender and all the liquid has been absorbed, about 20 minutes. Uncover and sprinkle in the lemon zest, dill and chives. Using a fork, fluff the rice, mixing in the zest and herbs. Cover to keep warm.

While the rice is cooking, prepare the salmon: In a sauté pan large enough to hold the salmon comfortably, combine the wine, the stock or clam juice, onion, carrot, celery, parsley, bay leaves and peppercorns. Bring to a boil, reduce the heat to low, cover and simmer for about 10 minutes to infuse the liquid.

Meanwhile, cut the salmon fillet crosswise into 8 equal strips; sprinkle with salt and white pepper. Gently roll up each strip into a tight coil and secure with a wooden skewer. Uncover the pan and arrange the salmon tournedos in the gently simmering liquid. Cover and poach just until the salmon is opaque throughout, 6–8 minutes.

As soon as the fish is ready, prepare the sauce: Strain ¼ cup (2 fl oz/60 ml) of the poaching liquid through a fine-mesh sieve into a food processor fitted with the metal blade. Add the roasted peppers and pulse several times to purée. With the motor running, pour in the oil in a thin, steady stream to form a thick, creamy consistency. Season to taste with salt and white pepper.

To serve, divide the rice among 4 individual serving dishes and spoon some of the sauce over each. Place 2 salmon tournedos on top of each serving and remove the skewers. Spoon a little more sauce over the top, garnish with parsley or dill and serve at once.

Serves 4

Sweet Sausage Patties

1 lb (500 g) lean ground (minced) pork

¼ cup (½ oz/15 g) fresh white bread crumbs

2 tablespoons low-fat milk

2 teaspoons pure maple syrup

2 teaspoons grated orange zest

2 teaspoons finely chopped fresh flat-leaf (Italian) parsley

½ teaspoon sweet paprika

½ teaspoon salt

½ teaspoon freshly ground pepper

Enjoy the taste of homemade breakfast sausage in a matter of minutes, without the excessive fat, salt or preservatives of many store-bought varieties. The sausage improves in flavor if refrigerated for 1–2 hours before cooking, and it may be stored for up to 2 days. For an interesting variation, try adding 1 teaspoon caraway or dill seeds. Or omit the maple syrup and spice up the mixture with 1 small fresh red or green chili pepper, seeded and minced.

*I*n a bowl, combine all the ingredients and, using your fingers, mix well. Divide into 12 equal portions.

Place a large nonstick frying pan over medium heat. Moisten your hands with water and gently pat each sausage portion into a patty about ½ inch (12 mm) thick and 2 inches (5 cm) in diameter. Working in batches if necessary, place the patties in the pan and fry, turning once, until cooked through and golden brown, about 5 minutes on each side. Remove from the pan and keep warm until all are cooked, then serve at once.

Serves 4–6

Smoked Salmon Hash

1¼ lb (625 g) white or red potatoes, unpeeled, cut into ½-inch (12-mm) dice

2 tablespoons unsalted butter

½ red (Spanish) onion, cut into ½-inch (12-mm) dice

1 green bell pepper (capsicum), seeded, deribbed and cut into ½-inch (12-mm) squares

14 oz (440 g) canned or vacuum-packed alder-smoked salmon, well drained, picked over to remove any errant bones and flaked by hand into ½-inch (12-mm) pieces

⅓ cup (3 fl oz/80 ml) half-and-half (half cream)

2 tablespoons grated lemon zest

2 tablespoons finely chopped fresh dill, plus dill sprigs for garnish

2 tablespoons finely chopped fresh chives

1 tablespoon finely chopped fresh flat-leaf (Italian) parsley

salt and ground white pepper

4 tablespoons (2 fl oz/60 ml) vegetable oil

This surprisingly delicate hash features alder-smoked salmon, available both in cans and in vacuum-packed pouches from specialty-food stores and well-stocked markets. The recipe also works well with regular canned salmon. Garnish with a dollop of sour cream, if desired.

Place the potatoes in a saucepan with lightly salted cold water to cover. Bring to a boil over high heat; reduce the heat to medium and simmer, uncovered, until just tender enough to pierce with a fork, 5–7 minutes.

Meanwhile, in a nonstick frying pan over medium heat, melt the butter. Add the red onion and bell pepper and sauté until tender-crisp, 4–5 minutes. Set aside.

Drain the potatoes and place in a bowl. Add the onion and pepper; set the frying pan aside and do not wash it. Add to the bowl the salmon, half-and-half, lemon zest, chopped dill, chives and parsley. Toss to mix well, taking care not to mash the potato pieces; season to taste with salt and white pepper and toss again.

Heat 2 tablespoons of the oil in the frying pan over medium heat. Add the hash mixture, pressing it down with a spatula to form an even, compact cake. Reduce the heat to medium-low and cook, shaking the pan occasionally, until crusty on the bottom, about 15 minutes. If the hash cake does not move freely, use the spatula to loosen the edges. Invert a large heatproof plate over the pan. Using oven mitts, firmly hold the pan and plate together and invert them. Lift off the pan.

Heat the remaining 2 tablespoons oil in the same pan and slide the hash cake, browned side up, back into it, tucking any stray pieces back into place. Cook until the second side is crusty, about 10 minutes longer. Unmold onto the same plate; cut into wedges and serve hot, garnished with dill sprigs.

Serves 4

Grilled Chicken Cobb Salad

FOR THE GRILLED CHICKEN:

4 boneless, skinless chicken breast
  halves, about 6 oz (185 g) each
2 tablespoons fresh lemon juice
2 tablespoons extra-virgin olive oil
1 teaspoon minced fresh rosemary
salt and freshly ground pepper

FOR THE DRESSING:

¼ cup (2 fl oz/60 ml) fresh lemon juice
½ teaspoon sugar
½ teaspoon salt
¼ teaspoon ground white pepper
1 tablespoon Dijon-style mustard
¾ cup (6 fl oz/180 ml) extra-virgin
  olive oil

FOR THE SALAD:

3 heads romaine (cos) lettuce, coarse
  outer leaves removed and remaining
  tender inner leaves coarsely chopped
8 slices smoked bacon, fried until crisp,
  drained and coarsely crumbled
3 hard-cooked eggs, coarsely chopped
6 oz (185 g) blue cheese, crumbled
3 firm but ripe plum (Roma) tomatoes,
  seeded and diced
1 large firm but ripe Hass avocado, halved,
  pitted, peeled and diced

2 tablespoons coarsely chopped fresh
  flat-leaf (Italian) parsley

*This variation on the traditional Cobb salad features quickly grilled
marinated chicken breast in place of cooked turkey breast.*

*T*o grill the chicken, one at a time, place each chicken breast
half between 2 sheets of plastic wrap. Using a rolling pin, roll
back and forth across the breast half until it is a uniform
thickness of about ½ inch (12 mm).

In a small bowl, stir together the lemon juice, olive oil and
rosemary. Place the chicken breasts in a shallow bowl large
enough to hold them in a single layer and pour the marinade
over them. Turn to coat evenly and let stand for 15–30 minutes.

Preheat a ridged stove-top grill pan over medium-high heat, or
preheat a broiler (griller).

While the grill pan or broiler preheats, make the dressing: In
another small bowl, stir together the lemon juice, sugar, salt and
pepper until the sugar and salt dissolve. Stir in the mustard until
blended. Beating continuously with a fork or small whisk, pour in
the oil in a thin, steady stream, and beat until emulsified. Set aside.

Season the chicken breasts with salt and pepper. Place on the
preheated grill pan, or slip under the broiler 3–4 inches (7.5–10
cm) from the heat source. Grill or broil, turning once, until just
opaque throughout, 2–3 minutes on each side.

While the chicken is grilling, combine the salad ingredients in
a large bowl and toss with just enough of the dressing to coat.
Arrange in individual bowls or on plates.

When the chicken is done, cut each breast half crosswise
into strips ½ inch (12 mm) wide and, keeping each breast half
together, arrange atop the salads. Spoon any remaining dressing
over the chicken, garnish with the parsley and serve.

Serves 4

Crab Meat and New Potato Salad with Lemon-Dill Dressing

1½ lb (750 g) red new potatoes
¼ cup (2 fl oz/60 ml) fresh lemon juice
1 teaspoon sugar
½ teaspoon salt
¼ teaspoon ground white pepper
2 tablespoons finely chopped fresh dill
¾ cup (6 fl oz/180 ml) extra-virgin
  olive oil
1 lb (500 g) cooked lump crab meat
2 heads butter (Boston) lettuce, leaves
  separated
fresh chervil leaves and sprigs

Surprisingly restrained in its flavors, this simple yet elegant salad is a lovely dish to serve for a special brunch. You can use precooked bay shrimp or even flaked canned tuna or salmon in place of the crab.

Place the potatoes in a large saucepan with lightly salted cold water to cover. Bring to a boil over medium-high heat; boil until tender enough to be pierced with the tip of a small, sharp knife, 10–15 minutes.

Meanwhile, make the dressing: In a bowl large enough to hold the potatoes, stir together the lemon juice, sugar, salt and white pepper until the sugar and salt dissolve. Stir in the dill. Beating continuously with a fork or small whisk, pour in the olive oil in a thin, steady stream, and beat until emulsified.

In another bowl, lightly toss the crab meat with 2 tablespoons of the dressing. Set aside.

As soon as the potatoes are done, drain them. Holding the hot potatoes with a folded kitchen towel to protect your hand and using a small, sharp knife, cut the potatoes, one at a time, into slices about ½ inch (12 mm) thick, letting the slices fall into the bowl of dressing. Toss the potatoes gently with the dressing and let stand at room temperature until tepid.

Arrange the lettuce leaves in a bed on a serving platter or individual plates. Spoon the potato salad on top of the leaves and arrange the crab meat on top of the potatoes. Garnish with chervil and serve at once.

Serves 6–8

Goat Cheese, Mushroom, Endive and Radicchio Salad

1 red bell pepper (capsicum)

2 heads radicchio, leaves separated

2 tablespoons sherry vinegar or
    balsamic vinegar

½ teaspoon salt

¼ teaspoon freshly ground pepper

1½ tablespoons Dijon-style mustard

¼ cup (2 fl oz/60 ml) walnut oil

¼ cup (2 fl oz/60 ml) olive oil

½ lb (250 g) creamy fresh goat cheese,
    in a log 1½–2 inches (4–5 cm) in
    diameter

2 heads Belgian endive (chicory/witloof),
    trimmed and thinly sliced crosswise

¼ lb (125 g) fresh mushrooms, thinly
    sliced

Beautiful and very satisfying, this stylish salad makes a great light brunch main course. Serve with hot crusty bread.

Preheat a broiler (griller). Cut the bell pepper lengthwise into quarters and remove the stem, seeds and ribs. Place cut sides down on a broiler pan and slip under the broiler 5–6 inches (13–15 cm) from the heat source. Broil (grill) until the skin is blistered and blackened. Remove from the broiler and cover with a piece of aluminum foil. Let cool for about 15 minutes; then, using your fingers or a small knife, peel away the blackened skin. Cut the pepper into long, thin strips. Set aside. Leave the broiler on.

Arrange the radicchio leaves attractively on individual salad plates to form cups. Set aside.

In a small bowl, stir together the vinegar, salt and pepper until the salt dissolves. Stir in the mustard. Beating continuously with a fork or small whisk, pour in the walnut and olive oils in a thin, steady stream, and beat until emulsified. Set aside.

Grease a flameproof baking dish with nonstick cooking spray. Cut the goat cheese into 4 equal rounds and place them in the prepared baking dish. Broil until golden brown, 2–3 minutes.

While the cheese is broiling, combine the endives and mushrooms in another bowl. Toss well with enough of the dressing to coat them evenly. Arrange the mixture in mounds atop the radicchio on each salad plate.

As soon as the cheese is done, use a spatula to transfer each round to a salad plate, placing it atop the endive-mushroom salad. Spoon a little more dressing on top and garnish with the roasted pepper strips. Serve at once.

Serves 4

Hot Shrimp Salad with Baby Spinach

¼ cup (1 oz/30 g) pine nuts

1 lb (500 g) medium-sized shrimp
  (prawns), peeled and deveined

8 cups (8 oz/250 g) loosely packed baby
  spinach leaves or large leaves torn into
  bite-sized pieces, carefully washed
  and dried

2 hard-cooked eggs, peeled and chopped

2 tablespoons fresh lemon juice

2 tablespoons balsamic vinegar

¾ teaspoon sugar

½ teaspoon salt, plus salt to taste

¼ teaspoon ground white pepper, plus
  white pepper to taste

2 teaspoons Dijon-style mustard

2 tablespoons finely chopped shallot

⅔ cup (5 fl oz/160 ml) extra-virgin
  olive oil

½ teaspoon red pepper flakes, optional

1 red bell pepper (capsicum), seeded,
  deribbed, roasted, peeled (*see glossary,
  page 104*) and cut into long, narrow
  strips

*A colorful and light brunch main course, this salad may also be
made with bay shrimp bought precooked, eliminating the step of
sautéing the shellfish.*

Put the pine nuts in a small, dry frying pan over medium-low
heat and toast, stirring continuously, until light golden brown,
3–5 minutes. Remove from the frying pan and set aside.

Meanwhile, put the shrimp in a bowl of lightly salted cold
water and let soak for 10–15 minutes. Rinse well with cool
running water, then drain thoroughly and pat dry.

Arrange the spinach leaves in beds on individual plates or in
shallow bowls. Scatter the eggs evenly on top. Set aside.

In a small bowl, stir together the lemon juice, vinegar, sugar,
½ teaspoon salt and ¼ teaspoon white pepper until the sugar
and salt dissolve. Stir in the mustard and shallot. Beating
continuously with a fork or small whisk, pour in all but 1
tablespoon of the olive oil in a thin, steady stream, and beat
until emulsified. Transfer the dressing to a small saucepan
and warm it over low heat. Keep warm.

In a large frying pan over medium heat, heat the remaining 1
tablespoon olive oil with the red pepper flakes, if using. Add
the shrimp to the pan, season lightly with salt and white pepper
and sauté, stirring, just until they turn pink, 1–2 minutes.

Arrange the shrimp attractively atop the beds of spinach.
Drizzle the hot dressing evenly over the shrimp and spinach
leaves. Garnish each salad with the bell pepper strips and pine
nuts and serve at once.

Serves 4

Creamy Vanilla French Toast

8 eggs
¼ cup (2 fl oz/60 ml) heavy (double)
  cream
1 teaspoon vanilla extract (essence)
8 thick slices good-quality white home-
  style bread, cut in half on the diagonal
4 tablespoons (2 oz/60 g) unsalted butter
confectioners' (icing) sugar
jam or pure maple syrup

A splash of cream and a hint of vanilla add richness to French toast. You can replace the vanilla with other favorite flavoring extracts, such as almond or rum. Decorative strips of orange peel and fresh mint sprigs make a nice garnish.

*I*n a large, shallow bowl, using a fork, beat the eggs until lightly frothy. Stir in the cream and vanilla.

Place the bread pieces in the bowl. Turn gently until they evenly soak up the egg mixture.

In a large frying pan or griddle over medium heat, melt 1 tablespoon of the butter. Add half of the bread pieces and fry until the undersides are golden brown, about 2 minutes. Cut 1 tablespoon of the butter into several pieces and add to the pan, distributing evenly; then flip the bread with a spatula and fry until the second sides are browned, about 2 minutes longer. Transfer to a warmed platter and keep warm until all are cooked. Repeat with the remaining bread and butter.

Place on warmed individual plates. Using a small fine-mesh sieve, lightly dust the tops with confectioners' sugar. Serve hot, with jam or maple syrup alongside.

Serves 4

Sourdough Pancakes with Blueberries

½ cup (4 fl oz/125 ml) sourdough starter, homemade *(recipe on page 11)* or store-bought

1½ cups (7½ oz/230 g) all-purpose (plain) flour

¼–½ cup (2–4 fl oz/60–125 ml) lukewarm water (110°F/43°C)

2 teaspoons sugar

1 teaspoon baking powder

1 teaspoon baking soda (bicarbonate of soda)

¼ teaspoon salt

1¼ cups (10 fl oz/310 ml) milk

1 egg, lightly beaten

1 tablespoon unsalted butter, melted, plus butter for cooking and serving

½ cup (2 oz/60 g) blueberries (fresh or frozen)

pure maple syrup

You can use sliced bananas in place of the blueberries, if you like.

*T*he night before you plan to cook the pancakes, begin preparing the batter: Put the sourdough starter in a bowl. Stir in ½ cup (2½ oz/75 g) of the flour and enough of the lukewarm water to form a pourable, creamy consistency. Cover lightly and leave overnight at room temperature; in the morning, the mixture should look bubbly and smell sour.

Measure out ½ cup (4 fl oz/125 ml) of the prepared sourdough mixture. If using homemade starter, stir the remaining sourdough mixture back into the starter base in the refrigerator. If using store-bought starter, follow the package directions.

In a bowl, stir together the remaining 1 cup (5 oz/155 g) flour, the sugar, baking powder, baking soda and salt. Make a well in the center and pour in the sourdough mixture, milk, egg and the melted butter. Starting at the center, gradually stir the ingredients together to form a smooth batter; do not overstir. Cover and let stand for 1 hour.

Preheat a large, heavy frying pan or griddle over medium heat and grease lightly with butter. Using a ¼-cup (2-fl oz/60-ml) measure, pour the batter onto the pan to form pancakes 6–7 inches (15–18 cm) in diameter. Immediately scatter 2 rounded teaspoons blueberries over each pancake. Cook until the surfaces are covered with bubbles and the edges start to look dry, 2–3 minutes. Flip the pancakes over; tuck in any stray berries. Cook until their undersides are golden, 1–2 minutes longer. Transfer to a warmed platter; repeat with the remaining batter and berries. Serve with butter and maple syrup.

Makes 12 pancakes; serves 4–6

Beaten Biscuits

2 cups (10 oz/315 g) all-purpose (plain) flour

1 tablespoon baking powder

1 teaspoon sugar

½ teaspoon salt

½ cup (4 oz/125 g) unsalted butter, chilled and cut into ½-inch (12-mm) pieces

¾ cup (6 fl oz/180 ml) whole or low-fat milk, chilled

A century or more ago, the dough for these rustic biscuits was actually beaten with a hammer, developing the flour's gluten to produce very crisp, flaky results. The action of a food processor's metal blades yields the same result, as well as beating in extra air that gives the biscuits a high rise. Serve with egg dishes, griddled ham or just butter and jam.

Preheat an oven to 425°F (220°C). Lightly butter 2 baking sheets.

In a food processor fitted with the metal blade, combine the flour, baking powder, sugar and salt. Pulse several times to combine. Add the butter and pulse again several times until the mixture resembles coarse crumbs. With the motor running, pour in the milk through the feed tube; continue processing just until the dough forms a ball.

Turn out the dough onto a lightly floured work surface and knead gently a few times. Pat it out to an even thickness of about ½ inch (12 mm). Using a round biscuit cutter 2 inches (5 cm) in diameter, cut out the biscuits. Arrange them evenly spaced on the prepared baking sheets.

Bake the biscuits until they are golden brown, 15–20 minutes. Serve hot.

Makes about 24 biscuits

Apple-Cinnamon Oatmeal

3–4 cups (24–32 fl oz/750 ml–1 l) water
  (see note)

½ teaspoon salt, optional

1 cup (3 oz/90 g) coarsely ground
  whole-grain oatmeal

2 large, crisp, sweet apples, halved and
  cored

1 teaspoon ground cinnamon

¼ cup (3 oz/90 g) honey, or to taste

A bowl of oatmeal is one of the healthiest breakfasts imaginable. Adding shredded apple and a dash of cinnamon complements the wonderfully earthy flavor of the grain. Seek out good stone-ground oats at a health-food store and follow the package directions for the precise proportion of water to oats and the necessary cooking time. If you wish to enrich the oatmeal, add pats of butter and some milk, half-and-half (half cream) or heavy (double) cream to individual servings.

*I*n a saucepan over high heat, bring the water to a rolling boil. Add the salt, if you like. Stirring continuously to prevent lumps from forming, stir in the oatmeal.

Reduce the heat to very low, cover the pan and cook until the oatmeal is thick and creamy, following the package direction's cooking time.

When the oatmeal is ready, uncover the pan and, using the large holes of a box grater/shredder, shred the apples directly into the pan. Sprinkle in the cinnamon and stir well.

Spoon the oatmeal into warmed individual bowls and drizzle evenly with the honey. Serve at once.

Serves 4

Cinnamon Pecan Streusel Coffee Cake

1¾ cups (9 oz/280 g) all-purpose (plain)
  flour
1¼ cups (10 oz/310 g) sugar
2 teaspoons baking powder
¼ cup (2 oz/60 g) unsalted butter, cut
  into pieces
1 egg, lightly beaten
¾ cup (6 fl oz/180 ml) milk
1 teaspoon vanilla extract (essence)
2 teaspoons ground cinnamon
½ cup (2 oz/60 g) coarsely chopped
  pecans

This classic coffee cake is excellent with the day's first mugful of coffee, as a midmorning snack, or cut into squares for a brunch buffet table. Substitute other nuts for the pecans, if you like.

Preheat an oven to 375°F (190°C). Butter an 8-inch (20-cm) square baking pan.

In a bowl, stir together the flour, 1 cup (8 oz/250 g) of the sugar and the baking powder. Using a pastry blender or 2 knives, cut in the butter until the mixture resembles coarse crumbs. Add the egg, milk and vanilla and stir until just blended. Pour the batter into the prepared pan.

In another bowl, stir together the remaining ¼ cup (2 oz/60 g) sugar, the cinnamon and pecans. Sprinkle the mixture evenly over the surface of the batter. Using a table knife, cut gently down through the batter at intervals of about 2 inches (5 cm) to spread a little of the topping through the batter.

Bake until the coffee cake is well risen and golden and a toothpick inserted into its center comes out clean, 25–30 minutes.

Remove from the oven and let cool on a rack for 15 minutes. Cut into squares and serve warm directly from the pan.

Serves 8–12

Breakfast Risotto

3 cups (24 fl oz/750 ml) unfiltered apple
   juice
2 cinnamon sticks, broken in half
pinch of ground nutmeg
2 cups (16 fl oz/500 ml) milk
2 tablespoons unsalted butter
1½ cups (10½ oz/330 g) Arborio rice
½ teaspoon salt
½ cup (3 oz/90 g) raisins
dark brown sugar
half-and-half (half cream)

Most people know risotto as a savory Italian side dish or main course that is customarily made with a plump, short-grain Italian rice variety known as Arborio. By using juice and milk in place of the traditional broth and wine, you will create a robust breakfast cereal that offers all the pleasures of rice pudding. Making risotto does require 30 minutes of constant attention, however, so you might want to make it the night before, refrigerate it, then reheat with a little more milk or juice.

*I*n a saucepan, combine the apple juice, cinnamon sticks and nutmeg. Bring to a boil over medium-high heat; immediately reduce the heat to low and keep warm. At the same time, in a separate saucepan, warm the milk over medium-low heat; turn off the heat, cover and keep warm.

In a large nonaluminum saucepan over medium-low heat, melt the butter. Add the rice and salt and stir with a wooden spoon until the rice begins to turn translucent, 2–3 minutes.

Ladle in about ½ cup (4 fl oz/125 ml) of the hot apple juice and stir the rice until it absorbs the juice. Continue adding the juice about ½ cup (4 fl oz/125 ml) at a time and stirring until absorbed. When all the juice has been added, ladle in about ½ cup (4 fl oz/125 ml) of the warm milk along with the raisins. Stir over medium-low heat until absorbed. Add the remaining milk in the same way, stirring after each addition until fully absorbed before adding more milk. All of the liquid will have been added and the rice will be tender in about 30 minutes. Test a few kernels for doneness; they should be creamy on the outside but *al dente* (tender but firm to the bite) at the center.

Remove the pan from the heat, cover and let stand for about 5 minutes. Ladle the risotto into warmed individual bowls. Pass the brown sugar and half-and-half at the table, to be added to taste.

Serves 4

Date-Nut Muffins

1 cup (8 fl oz/250 ml) water

1 cup (6 oz/185 g) date nuggets or chopped pitted dates

½ cup (4 oz/125 g) sugar

½ cup (4 oz/125 g) unsalted butter

½ teaspoon vanilla extract (essence)

2 eggs

2 cups (10 oz/315 g) all-purpose (plain) flour

2 teaspoons baking powder

¼ teaspoon baking soda (bicarbonate of soda)

¼ teaspoon salt

⅓ cup (1½ oz/45 g) chopped pecans

Although soaking the dates adds about 15 minutes to the overall preparation time, the result of this extra step is incredibly moist, tender muffins. Leave out the nuts, if you prefer, or substitute chopped walnuts or hazelnuts (filberts). Store in an airtight container at cool room temperature for up to 3 days, or freeze for up to several weeks.

*P*reheat an oven to 375°F (190°C). Butter a 12-cup muffin pan.

In a small saucepan over medium-high heat, bring the water to a boil. Stir in the dates, sugar and butter, remove from the heat and let stand until the dates have absorbed most or all of the liquid and have cooled to lukewarm, about 15 minutes.

Transfer the dates and any remaining liquid in the pan to a mixing bowl. Add the vanilla. One at a time, add the eggs, beating well with a wooden spoon after each addition until thoroughly incorporated. In another bowl, stir together the flour, baking powder, baking soda and salt. Add the date mixture and the nuts and stir just until well combined.

Spoon the batter into the prepared muffin-pan cups, filling each about three-fourths full. Bake until the muffins are well risen and a toothpick inserted into the center of one comes out clean, about 20 minutes.

Remove from the oven and let cool for 5 minutes in the pan, then remove the muffins from the pan. Serve warm or at room temperature.

Makes 12 muffins

French Toast Stuffed with Bananas and Walnuts

6 eggs
¼ cup (2 fl oz/60 ml) milk
4 very ripe bananas
¼ cup (1 oz/30 g) coarsely chopped
   walnuts
⅛ teaspoon freshly grated nutmeg
8 slices egg bread
4 tablespoons (2 oz/60 g) unsalted butter
confectioners' (icing) sugar
jam or pure maple syrup

Layering two slices of bread, sandwich style, with a mixture of bananas and walnuts results in French toast with a surprise filling. Try other favorite nuts in place of the walnuts, if you like. Accompany with bacon, ham or sausage.

*I*n a large, shallow bowl, using a fork, beat the eggs until lightly frothy. Stir in the milk. Set aside.

Peel the bananas into a small bowl and mash with a fork. Stir in the walnuts and nutmeg. Spread the banana-walnut mixture evenly over half the bread slices, leaving a ¼-inch (6-mm) border uncovered on all edges. Top with the remaining bread slices and press down gently to seal.

Place 2 sandwiches in the egg mixture. Turn gently until evenly saturated on both sides. Remove from the bowl and repeat with the remaining 2 sandwiches.

In a frying pan or griddle large enough to hold all the sandwiches at once, melt 2 tablespoons of the butter over medium heat. Add the sandwiches and fry until the undersides are golden brown, about 2 minutes. Add the remaining 2 tablespoons butter to the pan in several pieces, distributing evenly, then flip the sandwiches with a spatula and fry until the second sides are browned, about 2 minutes longer.

Place on warmed individual plates. Using a small fine-mesh sieve, lightly dust the tops with confectioners' sugar. Serve hot, with jam or maple syrup alongside.

Serves 4

Oven-Baked Dutch Apple Pancake

FOR THE APPLE FILLING:

2 tablespoons unsalted butter

3 large Granny Smith or other firm, tart apples, peeled, halved, cored and thinly sliced

6 tablespoons (3 oz/90 g) granulated sugar

1 teaspoon ground cinnamon

FOR THE PANCAKE:

3 eggs

½ cup (2½ oz/75 g) all-purpose (plain) flour

½ cup (4 fl oz/125 ml) milk

1 tablespoon sour cream

¼ teaspoon salt

1 teaspoon grated lemon zest

confectioners' (icing) sugar

Reminiscent of Pennsylvania Dutch cooking, this pancake is immensely satisfying for a weekend breakfast or brunch. You could also make a delicious plain pancake by baking the batter without the apples in a hot frying pan greased with butter. Either way, serve with ham or sausage.

Preheat an oven to 400°F (200°C).

To make the apple filling, in a 10-inch (25-cm) ovenproof frying pan over medium-high heat, melt the butter. Add the apples, sugar and cinnamon and sauté, stirring constantly, until the apples begin to soften and brown lightly, 3–5 minutes. Remove from the heat.

To make the pancake, in a bowl, using an electric mixer set on medium speed, beat the eggs until lightly frothy. Add the flour, milk, sour cream, salt and lemon zest and beat just until a smooth batter forms.

Immediately pour the batter over the apples in the hot pan and place in the oven. Bake until nicely puffed and golden brown, about 25 minutes.

Using a small fine-mesh sieve, lightly dust confectioners' sugar over the top. Serve directly from the pan, cut in half or into wedges.

Serves 2–4

Swiss Bircher Muesli

¾ cup (2 oz/60 g) old-fashioned rolled oats

½ cup (2 oz/60 g) coarsely chopped walnuts

¾ cup (6 oz/185 g) nonfat or low-fat plain yogurt

½ cup (4 fl oz/125 ml) nonfat milk, plus extra milk for serving

½ cup (3 oz/90 g) coarsely chopped dried apricots

2 crisp, sweet apples, halved and cored

¾ cup (4½ oz/140 g) seedless grapes, halved

honey

Muesli was originally formulated as a healthful, complete breakfast food at the alpine sanitorium of Dr. Bircher-Benner. Most recipes for the cold cereal call for the raw oats to be soaked overnight in water, then mixed with cream and fruit. In this version, they are toasted first, developing a more nutlike color, flavor and texture; then they are soaked in yogurt with dried fruit. Vary the mixture to your liking, using different dried and fresh fruits and nuts, and adding toasted sesame seeds or wheat germ, if you wish.

*T*he night before you plan to serve the muesli, begin preparing the oats: Preheat an oven to 325°F (165°C). Spread the oats on a baking sheet and toast them in the oven until golden brown, 15–20 minutes. Remove from the oven, transfer to a bowl and let cool.

Meanwhile, spread the nuts on the baking sheet and toast until lightly browned and fragrant, 8–10 minutes. Remove from the oven, let cool and set aside until the next day.

Add the yogurt and the ½ cup (4 fl oz/125 ml) milk to the oats and stir well. Stir in the dried apricots, then cover the bowl and refrigerate overnight.

The next morning, using the large holes of a box grater/shredder, shred the apples directly into the bowl. Add the grapes and nuts and stir well, being careful not to crush the grapes. Transfer to individual bowls. Pass honey and milk at the table to be added to taste.

Serves 4–6

Sourdough Waffles with Nuts

½ cup (4 fl oz/125 ml) sourdough
  starter, homemade (recipe on page 11)
  or store-bought
1½ cups (7½ oz/230 g) all-purpose
  (plain) flour
¼–½ cup (2–4 fl oz/60–125 ml)
  lukewarm water (110°F/43°C)
1 tablespoon sugar
½ teaspoon baking soda (bicarbonate
  of soda)
¼ teaspoon salt
1 egg, lightly beaten
1 cup (8 fl oz/250 ml) milk
½ cup (2 oz/60 g) small walnut pieces
pure maple syrup
fresh fruit, optional

This recipe yields enough waffles to feed 8 as part of a hearty breakfast; the precise number of waffles it makes will vary according to your waffle iron.

The night before you plan to cook the waffles, begin preparing the batter: Put the sourdough starter in a bowl. Stir in ½ cup (2½ oz/75 g) of the flour and enough of the lukewarm water to form a pourable, creamy consistency. Cover lightly and leave overnight at room temperature; in the morning, the mixture should look bubbly and smell sour.

Measure out ½ cup (4 fl oz/125 ml) of the prepared sourdough mixture. If using homemade starter, stir the remaining sourdough mixture back into the starter in the refrigerator. If using store-bought starter, follow the package directions.

In a bowl, stir together the remaining 1 cup (5 oz/155 g) flour, the sugar, baking soda and salt. Make a well in the center and pour in the sourdough mixture, egg and milk. Starting at the center, gradually stir the ingredients together to form a smooth batter; do not overstir. Cover and let stand for 1 hour.

Preheat an oven to 325°F (165°C). Spread the walnuts on a baking sheet and toast until lightly browned and fragrant, 8–10 minutes. Remove from the oven and set aside.

Preheat a waffle iron following the manufacturer's directions. Lightly grease the waffle iron and ladle in enough batter for 1 waffle; immediately scatter some walnuts over the batter. Close the waffle iron and cook until it opens easily or according to the manufacturer's directions; do not disturb for at least 2 minutes. Transfer to a warmed platter; repeat with the remaining batter. Serve with maple syrup and fruit, if desired.

Serves 8

Seven-Grain Buttermilk Pancakes

¾ cup (4 oz/125 g) all-purpose (plain) flour

½ cup (3 oz/90 g) seven-grain flour or seven-grain cereal

¼ cup (1¼ oz/37 g) unsalted shelled sunflower seeds, optional

1 tablespoon sugar

1½ teaspoons baking powder

½ teaspoon salt

1 cup (8 fl oz/250 ml) buttermilk

¼ cup (2 fl oz/60 ml) milk

2 tablespoons unsalted butter, melted, plus butter for cooking and serving

1 egg, lightly beaten

pure maple syrup or fruit spread

You'll find multigrain flour or slightly coarser-ground cereal in health-food stores or well-stocked markets. It doesn't matter whether you use four-grain or even ten-grain; seven-grain is called for here because it is among the most commonly available.

*I*n a bowl, stir together the all-purpose flour, seven-grain flour or cereal, sunflower seeds (if using), sugar, baking powder and salt. Make a well in the center and pour in the buttermilk, milk, melted butter and egg. Starting at the center, stir the ingredients together, gradually mixing in the dry ingredients to form a smooth batter; do not overstir. Cover and let stand at room temperature for 1 hour, or refrigerate overnight.

Preheat a large, heavy frying pan or griddle over medium heat and grease lightly with butter. Using a ¼-cup (2-fl oz/60-ml) measure, pour the batter onto the pan to form pancakes 6–7 inches (15–18 cm) in diameter. Cook until bubbles cover their surface, about 1 minute. Using a spatula, flip the pancakes and cook until browned on the undersides, about 1 minute longer. Transfer to a warmed platter and keep warm until all are cooked. Repeat with the remaining batter.

Serve hot with butter and maple syrup or fruit spread.

Makes about 12 pancakes; serves 4–6

Maple Polenta

¼ cup (1 oz/30 g) pine nuts, optional

5 cups (40 fl oz/1.25 l) low-fat milk

½ teaspoon salt

1 cup (5 oz/155 g) polenta

6 tablespoons (3 fl oz/90 ml) pure maple syrup

2 tablespoons unsalted butter, optional

¼ cup (1½ oz/45 g) seedless raisins, optional

¾ cup (6 fl oz/180 ml) milk, half-and-half (half cream) or heavy (double) cream, optional

Polenta, which is both the name of Italy's popular cornmeal and the robust porridge made from it, is usually eaten as a savory side dish. This recipe illustrates how good it can be as a hot breakfast cereal.

*I*f you would like to garnish the polenta with pine nuts, put them in a small, dry frying pan over medium-low heat and toast, stirring continuously, until light golden brown, 3–5 minutes. Remove from the frying pan and set aside.

In a saucepan over medium heat, combine the milk and salt and bring to a boil. Stirring continuously with a wooden spoon to prevent lumps from forming, pour in the polenta in a thin, steady stream. Reduce the heat to low and cook, stirring frequently, until the polenta is very thick, about 20 minutes.

Stir in the maple syrup and transfer to warmed individual bowls. Eat the polenta as it is, or top each serving with the butter, raisins, pine nuts and/or a drizzle of milk, half-and-half or cream.

Serves 4–6

Buttermilk Berry Crumble Coffee Cake

FOR THE CRUMBLE TOPPING:

¼ cup (2 oz/60 g) firmly packed dark brown sugar

2 tablespoons all-purpose (plain) flour

pinch of ground nutmeg

2 tablespoons unsalted butter

¼ cup (1¼ oz/37 g) chopped blanched almonds

¼ cup (¾ oz/20 g) old-fashioned rolled oats

FOR THE CAKE:

1½ cups (7½ oz/235 g) all-purpose (plain) flour

½ cup (4 oz/125 g) granulated sugar

½ teaspoon baking powder

¼ teaspoon baking soda (bicarbonate of soda)

¼ cup (2 oz/60 g) unsalted butter, cut into pieces

1 egg, lightly beaten

1 cup (8 fl oz/250 ml) buttermilk

½ teaspoon vanilla extract (essence)

1 cup (4 oz/125 g) raspberries or blueberries (fresh or frozen)

This delectable coffee cake has a rich, moist golden crumb that contrasts pleasantly with its juicy pockets of berries and crisp nut-and-oat topping. If available, try other berries such as whole blackberries or boysenberries or halved strawberries. Walnuts or pecans can stand in for the almonds.

Preheat an oven to 350°F (180°C). Butter an 8-inch (20-cm) square baking pan.

To make the crumble topping, in a small bowl, stir together the brown sugar, flour and nutmeg. Using a pastry blender or 2 knives, cut in the butter until the mixture resembles coarse crumbs. Mix in the almonds and oats. Set aside.

To make the cake, in a bowl, stir together the flour, granulated sugar, baking powder and baking soda. Using the pastry blender or 2 knives, cut in the butter until the mixture resembles fine crumbs. Add the egg, buttermilk and vanilla and stir just until blended.

Pour the batter into the prepared pan. Scatter the berries evenly over the surface. Sprinkle the crumble mixture evenly over the berries. Bake until the cake is well risen and golden and a wooden toothpick inserted into the center comes out clean, about 50 minutes.

Remove from the oven and let cool on a rack for 15 minutes. Cut into squares and serve warm directly from the pan.

Serves 8–12

Multibran Muffins with Golden Raisins

1½ cups (7½ oz/235 g) all-purpose (plain) flour

¼ cup (¾ oz/20 g) oat bran

¼ cup (¾ oz/20 g) rice bran

¼ cup (¾ oz/20 g) wheat bran

1 tablespoon baking powder

2 teaspoons grated orange zest

¼ teaspoon salt

1 cup (8 fl oz/250 ml) low-fat milk

½ cup (6 oz/185 g) honey

¼ cup (2 fl oz/60 ml) vegetable oil

1 egg, lightly beaten

½ cup (3 oz/90 g) golden raisins (sultanas)

In recent years, the widely reported health benefits of fiber in general and oat and other brans in particular have made bran muffins surge in popularity. This recipe features the three most widely available types of bran, all sold in well-stocked markets and health-food stores. Although all-purpose flour contributes tenderness, the high proportion of bran makes the muffins dry out fairly quickly; enjoy them fresh from the oven and freeze any remainders for up to several weeks.

Preheat an oven to 400°F (200°C). Butter a 12-cup muffin pan.

In a bowl, stir together the flour, brans, baking powder, orange zest and salt. Add the milk, honey, vegetable oil and egg and stir just until the batter is evenly moistened but still slightly lumpy. Add the raisins and fold in gently.

Spoon the batter into the prepared muffin-pan cups, filling each about two-thirds full. Bake until the muffins are well risen, golden brown and a wooden toothpick inserted into the center of one comes out clean, 18–20 minutes.

Remove from the oven and let cool for 5 minutes in the pan, then remove from the pan. Serve warm.

Makes 12 muffins

Citrus Segments in Vanilla Bean Syrup

1⅓ cups (11 fl oz/340 ml) water
⅔ cup (5 oz/155 g) sugar
1 vanilla bean, split in half lengthwise
4 large navel oranges
2 large grapefruits
fresh mint sprigs

A light, aromatic syrup highlights the vibrant taste of citrus fruit. This dish looks especially pretty made with pink or Ruby Red grapefruit. Try flavoring the syrup with 2 cinnamon sticks or 2 fresh mint sprigs instead of vanilla. This treatment also works very well with chunks of fresh pineapple or firm but ripe peaches or nectarines.

In a small saucepan, stir together the water and sugar; add the vanilla bean. Place over medium heat and bring to a simmer, stirring frequently to dissolve the sugar completely. Remove from the heat and let cool. Transfer the syrup to a bowl; discard the vanilla bean or save it for another use.

Section the oranges and grapefruits: Using a small, sharp knife, cut off a slice from both the stem and blossom ends of each fruit, removing all the membrane to reveal the flesh. Then stand the fruit upright and, following its contour, slice off the peel, pith and membrane in thick strips. Holding the fruit over the bowl of syrup to catch the juice, cut along the membrane on either side of each segment, letting the segments drop into the syrup. When sectioning the grapefruits, be sure to remove any seeds from the segments (loosen them with the tip of the knife), and then cut each segment in half to approximate the size of the orange segments before adding them to the syrup.

Using a spoon, gently toss the segments in the syrup until well coated. Cover and refrigerate until well chilled.

Serve in small chilled bowls, garnished with mint sprigs.

Serves 6

Meringue-Topped Baked Apples

6 large Granny Smith or other firm, tart
   apples
½ cup (4 fl oz/125 ml) unfiltered apple
   juice
⅔ cup (4 oz/125 g) raisins
½ cup (2 oz/60 g) coarsely chopped
   walnuts
½ cup (3½ oz/105 g) firmly packed
   dark brown sugar
½ teaspoon ground cinnamon
2 egg whites
pinch of cream of tartar
pinch of salt
¼ cup (2 oz/60 g) granulated sugar

*With just 5 minutes or so of extra work, simple baked apples become
an eye-catching morning dish with a topping of golden meringue.*

*P*reheat an oven to 350°F (180°C).

Using an apple corer or a paring knife, core each apple, cutting
to within ¾ inch (2 cm) of the bottom; do not pierce the bottom.
Trim off the peel and a little of the fruit from around the stem
area to give each apple a completely level top. Trim a little slice
off the bottom, if necessary, for it to stand upright. Using a small
spoon or the paring knife, scoop out a pocket about 1½ inches
(4 cm) wide and 2½ inches (6 cm) deep from the center. Stand
the apples upright in a shallow baking dish. Set aside.

In a small saucepan over medium heat, combine the apple
juice and raisins. Simmer gently, stirring occasionally, until the
raisins have absorbed most of the liquid, 6–8 minutes. Remove
from the heat and stir in the walnuts, brown sugar and cinnamon.

Spoon an equal amount of the raisin mixture into the center of
each apple. Pour water into the baking dish to a depth of about
¾ inch (2 cm). Bake until the apples are tender when pierced
with the tip of a knife, 45–60 minutes.

When the apples are almost done, place the egg whites in a
bowl. Using an electric mixer set on medium speed, beat until
blended. Add the cream of tartar and salt and continue beating
until white and foamy. Beating continuously, sprinkle in the
granulated sugar and beat until soft peaks form.

When the apples are done, carefully slide out the oven rack or
briefly remove the dish from the oven. Spoon an equal amount
of the egg whites on top of each apple. Continue baking until
the meringue is golden brown, about 5 minutes longer. Serve
hot, warm or at room temperature.

Serves 6

Fresh Fruit and Lemon Curd Tart

basic quiche and tart pastry *(recipe on page 12)*

1 cup (10 oz/315 g) prepared lemon curd *(see note)*

1½–2 cups (6–10 oz/185–315 g) mixed whole berries, citrus segments and sliced juicy fresh fruit *(see note)*

fresh mint sprigs, optional

The ideal finish to a weekend brunch, this tart is simplicity itself, made even simpler by using prepared lemon curd sold in jars in well-stocked markets and specialty-food stores. Comb the produce section for an attractive array of fresh, juicy fruits, including all kinds of berries, kiwifruits, tangerines and clementines, blood oranges, peaches, nectarines and plums, for arranging in the tart shell.

*P*reheat an oven to 425°F (220°C).

Using a rolling pin, roll out the pastry dough on a lightly floured work surface into a round 12 inches (30 cm) in diameter. Drape the round over the rolling pin and carefully transfer to a 9-inch (23-cm) tart pan with removable bottom. Undrape the pastry and gently ease it into the bottom and sides of the pan. Trim the pastry even with the pan rim.

Prick the bottom and sides of the pastry shell with the tines of a fork. Form a double-thick 12-inch (30-cm) square of aluminum foil, poke a few holes in it, then press it snugly into the pastry-lined pan. Bake for 4 minutes. Remove the foil and continue baking until the pastry looks crisp and golden brown, 8–10 minutes longer. Transfer to a rack and let cool.

When the tart shell is cool, remove the pan rim and place the tart shell on a serving plate. Spread the lemon curd evenly over the bottom of the tart shell, arrange the fruit in an attractive pattern on top and garnish with mint sprigs, if desired. Serve at once, or refrigerate for up to 1 hour before serving.

Makes one 9-inch (23-cm) tart; serves 6–8

Banana-Berry Smoothies

¾ cup (6 fl oz/180 ml) buttermilk
½ cup (4 oz/125 g) nonfat vanilla
  yogurt
½ banana, peeled and cut into chunks
3 strawberries, hulled
2 teaspoons honey
2 ice cubes

The smoothie has successfully made the transition from a health fad to an everyday nourishing and delicious quick breakfast in a glass. Possible variations are countless. Try it with any soft, juicy fruit, including mango, papaya, pineapple, peach or nectarine. Low-fat or nonfat milk may replace the buttermilk.

Put the buttermilk, yogurt, banana, berries and honey in a blender. Cover and blend at high speed until smooth.

  With the motor running, add the ice cubes, one at a time, and continue blending until smooth and frothy. Pour into 1 or 2 large chilled glasses. Serve at once.

Serves 1 or 2

Light Bananas Foster with Frozen Yogurt

1 pint (16 fl oz/500 ml) low-fat vanilla
   frozen yogurt
¼ cup (1 oz/30 g) pecan pieces
¼ cup (2 oz/60 g) unsalted butter, cut
   into small pieces
½ cup (3½ oz/105 g) firmly packed
   light brown sugar
4 large, ripe bananas, peeled, halved
   lengthwise, and each half cut in half
   crosswise
½ teaspoon ground cinnamon
2 tablespoons grated orange zest
pinch of ground nutmeg
½ cup (4 fl oz/125 ml) banana-flavored
   liqueur
½ cup (4 fl oz/125 ml) light rum

This version of the classic Sunday brunch finale from Brennan's restaurant in New Orleans lightens the fat without stinting on the flavor. Make it just before serving time.

An hour or so before serving, scoop the frozen yogurt into attractive individual dishes and put them in the freezer to chill.

Preheat an oven to 325°F (165°C). Spread the pecans on a baking sheet and toast until lightly browned and fragrant, 8–10 minutes. Remove from the oven and let cool.

In a nonstick frying pan over medium-low heat, melt the butter with the brown sugar, stirring continuously. When the mixture develops a syrupy consistency, after 3–5 minutes, add the bananas. Cook, continually spooning the syrup over the bananas, until the fruit is heated through, about 5 minutes. Sprinkle the cinnamon, orange zest and nutmeg over the bananas and stir gently to combine.

Bring the chilled dishes of frozen yogurt to the table, then immediately pour the banana liqueur and rum into the frying pan. Stir briefly to combine the liquors with the sauce and to warm them through. Carefully carry the pan to the table and set it securely on a trivet. With a long kitchen match, ignite the sauce. As soon as the flames die, spoon the bananas and sauce over the frozen yogurt. Garnish with the pecans.

Serves 4

Spiced Dried Fruit Compote

1 cup (6 oz/185 g) packed dried apricots
1 cup (6 oz/185 g) packed dried peaches
1 cup (6 oz/185 g) packed dried pears
1 cup (6 oz/185 g) packed dried pitted
   prunes
1 cup (6 oz/185 g) raisins
¾ cup (6 oz/185 g) sugar
6 whole cloves
2 cinnamon sticks, broken in half
4 whole peppercorns
1 whole star anise
1 lemon zest strip, about 3 inches
   (7.5 cm) long and ½ inch (12 mm) wide

Chinese star anise adds a subtle, exotic taste to this winter breakfast or brunch dish.

*I*n a saucepan, combine all the ingredients. Add cold water to cover the fruits by about ½ inch (12 mm).

Cover and bring to a boil over medium-high heat. Reduce the heat to very low and simmer gently, stirring occasionally, until the fruits are plumped and tender, about 30 minutes. Remove from the heat.

Serve warm, at room temperature or chilled. To serve chilled, let cool, cover and refrigerate until cold, 2–3 hours, or for up to 3 days. Before serving, take care to remove all the whole spices.

Serves 6–8

Broiled Grapefruit

2 large grapefruits, well chilled
½ cup (3½ oz/105 g) firmly packed
   light brown sugar
2 tablespoons unsalted butter, melted
1 teaspoon ground cinnamon
4 small fresh mint sprigs

The pleasures of broiled grapefruit are akin to those of a classic crème brûlée, only here the hot caramelized topping gives way to cool, tart-sweet segments of citrus fruit instead of chilled custard. Any grapefruit variety will work in this recipe; just be sure the fruits are well chilled to produce the best results.

*P*reheat a broiler (griller).

Cut each grapefruit in half crosswise. Cut a thin slice off the bottom of each half, if necessary, so that it will stand upright.

Using a serrated grapefruit knife or a small, sharp knife, loosen the grapefruit segments in each half by first carefully cutting between the fruit and the peel and then by cutting along either side of each segment to free it from its membrane. Leave all the segments in their shells. Place the halves upright in a baking dish.

In a small bowl, stir together the sugar, butter and cinnamon. Using your fingers, sprinkle the sugar mixture evenly over the grapefruit halves. Slip under the broiler about 4 inches (10 cm) from the heat source and broil (grill) until the sugar is uniformly bubbly, 2–3 minutes.

Transfer each grapefruit half to an individual dish and garnish with a mint sprig. Serve at once.

Serves 4

Melon Balls with Crystallized Ginger and Honey

½ large, ripe cantaloupe
½ large, ripe honeydew melon
2 tablespoons finely chopped
  crystallized ginger
1 tablespoon honey
1½ teaspoons fresh lime juice
fresh mint leaves

Ginger brings out the exotic perfume of fresh melon. For a more colorful effect, use a mixture of two or more different kinds of melon; any good, juicy, sweet variety—apart from watermelon—will work well. Try substituting 1 tablespoon peeled and finely grated fresh ginger for the crystallized variety. For a particularly beautiful presentation, slip a few lime slices into each bowl just before serving.

Remove any seeds from the melon halves. Using a melon baller, scoop out balls from the melons and place them in a bowl. Sprinkle the balls with the crystallized ginger, then drizzle with the honey and add the lime juice. Using a large spoon, toss gently until well mixed. Cover and refrigerate for 1 hour.

Just before serving, gently stir the fruit to mix it with the ginger and juices that have collected in the bottom of the bowl. Spoon the fruits, along with their juices, into chilled individual bowls. Garnish with mint leaves and serve cold.

Serves 4

Mashed Potato Cakes

1 lb (500 g) Yukon Gold or other waxy
   yellow potatoes, unpeeled, quartered
2 tablespoons unsalted butter, at room
   temperature
2 tablespoons milk
½ small yellow onion, grated
2 eggs, lightly beaten
2 tablespoons freshly grated Parmesan
   cheese
½ teaspoon salt
¼ teaspoon freshly ground pepper
1 cup (4 oz/125 g) fine dried bread
   crumbs
¼ cup (2 fl oz/60 ml) vegetable oil

*Although this recipe starts from scratch with uncooked potatoes, you
can also use leftover mashed potatoes. You'll need about 2 cups (1 lb/
500 g) cold mashed potatoes; if they've already been enriched with
butter and milk, omit those ingredients when you prepare the cake
mixture. Serve with eggs or as an accompaniment to grilled sausages.*

Place the potatoes in a saucepan with lightly salted cold water
to cover. Bring to a boil over high heat; reduce the heat to
medium and simmer, uncovered, until the potatoes are tender
when pierced with a fork, 10–12 minutes. Drain well. Purée
the potatoes by pressing them through a ricer placed over a
bowl, or peel the potatoes, place in a bowl and mash until
smooth with a hand-held potato masher.

Stir in the butter, then add the milk, onion and eggs and stir
until blended. Add the Parmesan, salt and pepper and stir again
until well mixed. Cover and refrigerate until the mixture is well
chilled and firm, at least 2 hours or for up to 24 hours.

Spread the bread crumbs on a plate. Heat the oil in a large
nonstick frying pan over medium heat.

While the oil is heating, using a ⅓-cup (2½-oz/75-g) measure,
scoop up a portion of the potato mixture and set it atop the
crumbs. Pat it down to a thickness of about ½ inch (12 mm)
and turn to coat evenly with crumbs on both sides. Transfer the
potato cake to the hot oil to begin frying while you shape and
coat the remaining mixture in the same way.

Working in batches if necessary, fry the potato cakes, turning
once, until golden brown, 2–3 minutes on each side. Using a
slotted spatula, transfer to paper towels to drain briefly.

Place on a warmed platter or individual plates and cover to
keep warm until all are cooked. Serve hot.

Makes 8 cakes; serves 6–8

Diner-Style Hash Browns

2½ lb (1.25 kg) boiling potatoes,
   unpeeled, quartered
salt and freshly ground pepper
2 tablespoons unsalted butter
2 tablespoons vegetable oil
2 tablespoons finely chopped fresh
   chives or parsley

Technically speaking, hash browns are diced. But most restaurants actually make them with shredded potatoes, a technique used here. The hash browns can also be cooked in a nonstick frying pan or formed into patties. If you like, add some grated yellow onion with the salt and pepper. For a glorious side dish, top the finished hash browns with shredded Cheddar cheese, sour cream and a favorite fresh salsa.

Place the potatoes in a saucepan with lightly salted cold water to cover. Bring to a boil over high heat. Reduce the heat to medium and simmer, uncovered, until parboiled, no more than 5 minutes; they should be barely tender when pierced with a fork. Drain well and set aside until cool enough to handle. Shred the potatoes on the large holes of a box grater/shredder held over a mixing bowl. Toss lightly with a little salt and pepper to taste.

On a nonstick griddle over medium heat, melt the butter with the vegetable oil. When the butter melts and begins to foam, spread it and the oil evenly over the surface of the griddle and place the shredded potatoes on top. With the back of a spatula, gently press down on the potatoes to form a compact, even mass 1–1½ inches (2.5–4 cm) thick. Do not be concerned if the edges are uneven. Fry until the underside is browned and crusty, about 5 minutes. Using the spatula, turn the cake over; you may turn the cake in sections if necessary. Continue frying until browned and crusty on the second side, 4–5 minutes longer.

Transfer the potatoes to a warmed serving platter or individual plates and garnish with chives or parsley. Serve at once.

Serves 6–8

Mixed Grill–Style Broiled Tomatoes

1 cup (2 oz/60 g) fresh white bread
   crumbs
4 large, firm but ripe plum (Roma)
   tomatoes
¼ cup (1 oz/30 g) freshly grated
   Parmesan cheese
3 tablespoons unsalted butter, melted
1½ teaspoons finely chopped fresh
   chives
1½ teaspoons finely chopped fresh
   flat-leaf (Italian) parsley
1 teaspoon finely chopped fresh tarragon
1 egg, lightly beaten
salt and freshly ground pepper

Old-fashioned English breakfasts always include these stuffed tomatoes alongside the traditional mixed grill of sausage, bacon and other breakfast meats. They also make an outstanding garnish for your favorite breakfast eggs.

*P*reheat a broiler (griller).

   In a flameproof baking dish large enough to hold the tomatoes, spread the bread crumbs in a thin, even layer. Slip the dish under the broiler about 4 inches (10 cm) from the heat source and broil (grill) until toasted to a light golden brown, 30–60 seconds. Remove from the broiler but leave the broiler on. Empty the crumbs into a bowl and set the baking dish aside.

   Core the tomatoes and cut them in half through their stem ends. Using a fingertip or the handle of a small spoon, remove their seeds and the pulp between the seed sacs.

   Add the Parmesan cheese, butter, chives, parsley, tarragon and egg to the toasted crumbs and stir to mix well. Season to taste with salt and pepper and mix well again.

   Spoon the bread crumb mixture into the tomato halves, dividing it evenly and mounding it slightly. Lightly grease the reserved baking dish and place the stuffed tomato halves in it, stuffing side up. Slip the dish under the broiler 8–10 inches (20–25 cm) from the heat source and broil (grill) until the tomatoes are hot and the stuffing is nicely browned, 5–7 minutes.

   Remove from the broiler and serve hot.

Serves 4

Glossary

The following glossary defines terms both generally and specifically as they relate to breakfast and brunch dishes, including major and unusual ingredients and basic techniques.

BACON
A cured pork product, bacon is first salted with a brine or dry salt to give it a drier, firmer texture, then usually smoked to give it a more robust flavor. Most bacon, sold in long, thin strips streaked with layers of meat and fat, comes from the belly section. In contrast, Canadian bacon (below) is cut from the center loin, a cylindrical cut noted for its leanness.

BAKING POWDER
Commercial baking product combining three ingredients: **baking soda,** the source of the carbon-dioxide gas that causes pancake, waffle, muffin and coffee cake batters to rise; an acid, such as cream of tartar, calcium acid phosphate or sodium aluminum sulphate, which, when the powder is combined with a liquid, causes the baking soda to release its gas; and a starch such as cornstarch (cornflour), to keep the powder from absorbing moisture.

BAKING SODA
Also known as bicarbonate of soda or sodium bicarbonate, the active component of **baking powder** and the source of the carbon-dioxide gas that leavens batters. Often used in combination with acidic ingredients such as **buttermilk, yogurt** or citrus juices.

BELL PEPPERS
Fresh, sweet-fleshed, bell-shaped member of the pepper family. Also known as capsicum. Most common in the unripe green form, although ripened red or yellow varieties are also available. Pale yellow, orange and purple types may also be found.

To prepare a raw bell pepper, cut it lengthwise into quarters. Pull out the stem section from each quarter, along with the cluster of seeds attached to it. Remove any remaining seeds, along with any thin white membranes, or ribs. Cut the pepper quarters as directed in each recipe.

To roast and peel a bell pepper, prepare pepper quarters as directed above and place them cut-sides down on a broiler pan. Broil (grill) about 4 inches (10 cm) below the heat source until the skins are evenly blackened and blistered. Remove from the broiler, cover with aluminum foil and let stand for 10 minutes, then peel away the skins.

BRANS
The papery brown coating of a whole grain, usually removed during milling. Unless the type of grain is specified, the term usually refers to wheat bran, also sometimes known as miller's bran. Included in batter mixtures, it provides robust flavor and texture, as well as a generous measure of dietary fiber. Oat and rice brans are also commonly available.

BREAD CRUMBS
To make fresh bread crumbs, choose a good-quality, rustic-style loaf made of unbleached wheat flour, with a firm, coarse-textured crumb. Cut away the crusts and break the bread into coarse chunks. Put them in a food processor fitted with the metal blade and process to desired consistency.

Purchase prepackaged dried crumbs in food stores, or make them from fresh crumbs; spread the fresh crumbs in a baking pan and bake in an oven set at its lowest temperature until dry but not brown, 30–60 minutes.

BUTTERMILK
Form of cultured low-fat or non-fat milk that contributes a tangy flavor and thick, creamy texture to batters and doughs, as well as to smoothies. Its acidity, when combined with leavening agents such as **baking soda,** adds extra lightness to batters.

CHEESES
For the best selection and finest quality, buy cheeses from a well-stocked food store or delicatessen that offers a wide range of choices and has a frequent turnover of product. Some used in this book are:

Blue Cheese Blue-veined cheeses of many types have rich, tangy flavors and creamy to crumbly consistencies. Widely available, high-quality examples include French Roquefort, Italian Gorgonzola and American Maytag blue (at left).

Cheddar Firm, smooth-textured whole-milk cheese, pale yellow-white to deep yellow-orange. Available in many varieties, all ranging in taste from mild and sweet when fresh to rich and sharply tangy when aged.

Goat Cheese Most cheeses made from goat's milk are fresh and creamy, with a distinctive sharp tang. They are generally sold shaped into small rounds or logs, some of which are coated with pepper, ash or an herb mixture that mildly flavors them. Also known by the French term *chèvre.*

Gruyère Variety of Swiss cheese with a smooth texture, small holes and mildly strong flavor.

Jarlsberg Norwegian cheese resembling Swiss Emmenthaler, but with a slightly sweeter taste.

Parmesan Hard, thick-crusted Italian cow's milk cheese with a sharp, salty, full flavor resulting from at least two years of aging. Buy in block form, to grate fresh as needed.

CORNED BEEF
Beef brisket, or sometimes other cuts, cured for about a month in a brine containing large crystals ("corns") of salt, along with sugar, spices and other seasonings and preservatives, to produce a meat that, when slowly simmered in water, develops a moist, tender texture, mildly spiced flavor and bright purplish red color.

CRAB MEAT
Precooked crab meat is widely available in fish markets or the seafood counters of quality food markets. Most often, it has been frozen; for best flavor and texture, seek out fresh crab meat. When fresh crab is in season (generally September–April), fish markets often sell cooked whole crabs; ask for them to be cracked, so that, once home, you can easily open the shells by hand and remove the meat. Left in coarse chunks, the shelled meat, particularly from the body of the crab, is known as lump crab meat; finer particles from the legs or broken down from larger lumps is known as "flaked" crab meat. Avoid imitation crab meat (surimi).

DATE NUGGETS
The sweet, deep brown fruit of the date palm tree has a thick, sticky consistency that resembles candied fruit. For convenience in baking, the fruit is formed into small, cylindrical nuggets and sold in the baking section of well-stocked markets. If unavailable, substitute chopped dates.

DRIED FRUIT
Intensely flavored and satisfyingly chewy, many forms of sun-dried or kiln-dried fruits may be added to breakfast breads and cereals to enhance their taste or texture. Select recently dried and packaged fruits, which have a softer texture than older dried fruits. Some of the most popular options, used in this book, include:

Apricots Pitted whole or halved fruits; sweet and slightly tangy.

Peaches Halved or quartered, pitted and flattened fruits; sweet and slightly tangy.

Pears Halved, seeded and flattened fruits, retaining the fresh pear's distinctive profile.

Prunes Variety of dried plum, with a rich-tasting, dark, fairly moist flesh.

Raisins Variety of dried grape, popular as a snack on their own. Both seedless dark raisins and golden raisins (sultanas) are used in baking and breakfast cereals.

FLOUR, SEVEN-GRAIN
A blend of finely ground grains—usually but not always wheat, corn, oats, rye, millet, rice and buckwheat—used to give robust, complex taste and texture to breakfast pancakes, waffles and baked goods. Blends of fewer or more types of grain may be substituted, as may slightly coarser-textured multigrain cereals intended for cooking and serving hot.

GINGER, CRYSTALLIZED
Small pieces of the rhizome of the tropical ginger plant, first preserved and then coated with granulated sugar. Also called candied ginger. Available in specialty-food shops, or the baking sections or Asian food sections of well-stocked stores.

HALF-AND-HALF
A commercial dairy product consisting of half milk and half light cream. In Britain, known as half cream.

HAM, SMOKED
The large, hind leg cut of pork is often cured whole with salt or brine and sugar, then smoked to enhance its flavor and texture. For the best quality, seek out country-style hams, which are cured with salt or brine and other seasonings, then smoked and cooked partially or completely before sale. If possible, buy smoked ham freshly sliced at the meat or delicatessen counter, rather than presliced.

HONEY
The natural, sweet, syruplike substance produced by bees from flower nectar, honey subtly reflects the color and flavor of

---

HERBS
Many savory breakfast dishes call for the addition of fresh and dried herbs. Some popular varieties, used in this book, include:

Basil Sweet, spicy herb popular in Italian and French cooking.

Bay Leaf Dried whole leaf of the bay laurel tree, pungent and spicy. Discard the leaves before serving.

Chervil Herb with small leaves resembling flat-leaf (Italian) parsley and with a subtle flavor reminiscent of both parsley and anise. Used fresh or dried.

Chive Long, thin green shoot with a mild flavor reminiscent of the onion, to which it is related. Although chives are available dried in the herb-and-spice section of food stores, fresh chives possess the best flavor.

Dill Fine, feathery leaves with a sweet, aromatic flavor. Used fresh or dried.

Mint Refreshing herb available in many varieties, with spearmint the most common. Used fresh to flavor a broad range of savory and sweet dishes.

Parsley This popular fresh herb is available in two varieties, the common curly-leaf type and a flat-leaf type (below). The latter, also known as Italian parsley, has a more pronounced flavor and is preferred.

Rosemary
Mediterranean herb, used fresh or dried, with an aromatic flavor well suited to a wide range of foods. Strong in flavor, it should be used sparingly, except when grilling.

Tarragon Fragrant, distinctively sweet herb used fresh or dried as a seasoning for eggs, vegetables, salads, seafood, chicken and light meats.

the blossoms from which it was made. Milder varieties, such as clover and orange blossom, are lighter in color and better suited to general cooking purposes. Those derived from herb blossoms have a more aromatic taste.

MAPLE SYRUP
Syrup made from boiling the sap of the maple tree. It has an inimitably rich savor, intense sweetness and caramel color. Select only those products labeled pure maple syrup; those lightest in color, often designated fancy or grade A, are the highest in quality.

MUSTARD
Mustard is available in three basic forms: whole seeds; powdered, often referred to as dry mustard; and prepared. Of the prepared types, true Dijon mustard and non-French blends labeled Dijon-style are pale in color and fairly hot and sharp tasting.

OATS
Oats are prized for their nutlike taste and texture when cooked as a breakfast porridge or added to baked goods. Coarse, medium or fine oatmeal is ground from hulled oats. Old-fashioned rolled oats (below) are flakes made from oats that have been cleaned and hulled, then flattened by passing them through heated rollers. Look for them in the baking or cereal sections of food stores.

OILS
Oils not only provide a medium in which foods may be browned without sticking, but can also

NUTS
A wide variety of nuts complement breakfast and brunch dishes, particularly pancakes, waffles and baked goods. Some of the most popular options, used in this book, include:

Almonds Mellow, sweet nuts popular throughout the world. Widely available whole, sliced, slivered and blanched—that is, with their skins removed.

Pecans Brown-skinned, crinkly textured nuts with a distinctive sweet, rich flavor and crisp, slightly crumbly texture. Native to the southern United States.

Pine Nuts Small, ivory seeds with a rich, slightly resinous flavor; extracted from the cones of a species of pine tree.

Walnuts Rich, crisp nuts with distinctively crinkled surfaces. English walnuts, the most familiar variety, are grown worldwide, although the largest crops are in California.

subtly enhance the flavor of many dishes and add tenderness to breakfast breads.

Olive Oil Extra-virgin olive oil is extracted from olives on the first pressing without use of heat or chemicals. It is prized for its pure, fruity taste and golden to pale green hue. Pure olive oil is less aromatic and flavorful; it may be used for all-purpose cooking.

Vegetable and Seed Oils Common varieties include safflower, canola and corn oil. All are employed for their high cooking temperatures and bland flavor.

Walnut Oil Rich-tasting oil offering a flavor reminiscent of the nuts from which it is pressed. Seek out oil made from lightly toasted nuts, which has a full but not too assertive flavor.

POTATOES
As accompaniments to eggs and as an essential ingredient in hashes, potatoes are a popular breakfast and brunch ingredient.

New Potatoes Any variety of potato harvested in early summer when small and immature. As a result, their flesh is sweet and tender. Most are red skinned, although tan-skinned new potatoes can also be found.

Waxy Yellow Potatoes Small-to-medium-sized potatoes prized for their waxy texture and rich flavor. The variety known as Yukon Gold has a deep yellow color and rich, almost buttery taste.

White Boiling Potatoes Medium-sized potatoes with thin tan skins. When cooked, their textures are finer than baking potatoes but coarser than waxy yellow varieties.

PROSCIUTTO
Italian-style raw ham, a specialty of the Tuscan town of Parma, cured by dry-salting for one month,

followed by air-drying in cool curing sheds for half a year or longer.

SALMON
With its rich, sweet flavor and tender texture, salmon enjoys special popularity as a breakfast and brunch fish. Buy fresh salmon from a reputable fishmonger; cuts taken from the center of the fillet are particularly meaty and most likely to be free of errant bones. Purchase cold-smoked salmon freshly sliced from a good-quality delicatessen or fish market. Lox, or salt-cured salmon, and Nova, another type of cold-smoked salmon, are commonly sold in Jewish delicatessens; they have oilier textures than smoked salmon and in most cases are not acceptable substitutes. Rich-tasting alder-smoked salmon, which is hot smoked over the fragrant wood of the alder tree, has a firmer, drier consistency due to the fact that it cooks as it is cured; it is sold in cans and vacuum-sealed pouches in well-stocked markets and specialty-food stores.

SHALLOTS
Small member of the onion family with brown skin, white-to-purple flesh and a flavor resembling a cross between sweet onion and garlic.

SHRIMP
Shrimp (prawns) are popular additions to omelets, quiches and other

savory breakfast and brunch dishes. Tiny bay shrimp are sold already cleaned, peeled and cooked at fishmongers and well-stocked markets. Raw shrimp are generally sold with the heads already removed but the shells still intact. Before cooking, they are usually peeled and their thin, veinlike intestinal tracts removed.

To peel and devein shrimp, use your thumbs to split open the shrimp's thin shell along the concave side, between its two rows of legs. Grasp the shell and gently peel it away. Using a small knife, make a shallow slit along the peeled shrimp's back, just deep enough to expose the long, usually dark, veinlike intestinal tract. Lift up and pull out the vein and discard it.

SUGAR
Many different forms of sugar may be used to sweeten breakfast and brunch dishes.

Brown Sugar A rich-tasting granulated sugar combined with molasses in varying quantities to yield golden, light or dark brown sugar, with crystals varying from coarse to fine.

Confectioners' Sugar Finely pulverized sugar, also known as powdered or icing sugar, which dissolves quickly and provides a thin, white decorative coating. To prevent confectioners' sugar from absorbing moisture in the air and caking, manufacturers often mix a little cornstarch into it.

Granulated Sugar The standard, widely used form of pure white sugar. Do not use superfine granulated (castor) sugar unless specified in the recipe.

TOMATOES
During summer, when tomatoes are in season, use the best red or yellow sun-ripened tomatoes you can find. At other times of year, plum tomatoes (below), sometimes called Roma or egg tomatoes, often have the best flavor and texture.

To seed a tomato, cut it in half crosswise. Squeeze gently to force out the seed sacs.

VANILLA
Vanilla beans are the dried aromatic pods of a variety of orchid. One of the most popular flavorings in baking and dessert making, vanilla is most commonly used in the form of an alcohol-based extract (essence). Be sure to purchase products labeled pure vanilla extract. Vanilla extract or beans from Madagascar are the best.

YEAST, ACTIVE DRY
One of the most widely available forms of yeast for baking, commonly sold in individual packages containing about 2½ teaspoons and found in the baking section of food stores. Seek out one of the new strains of quick-rise yeast available in specialty-food stores.

YOGURT
Milk fermented by bacterial cultures that impart a mildly acidic flavor and custardlike texture. So-called plain yogurt refers to the unflavored product, to distinguish it from the many popular varieties of flavored and sweetened yogurt. Unpasteurized yogurt contains live yogurt cultures, which may be used to start your own home-made yogurt. Available made from whole, low-fat or nonfat milk; for the recipes in this book, use whichever type you prefer, depending upon taste and dietary needs.

ZEST
Thin, brightly colored, outermost layer of a citrus fruit's peel, containing most of its aromatic essential oils—a lively source of flavor. Zest may be removed in thin strips using a simple tool known as a zester (below), its sharp-edged holes drawn across the fruit's skin, or in small particles with a fine hand-held grater.

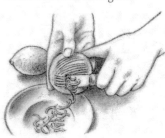

SPICES
Spices enliven both sweet and savory breakfast and brunch dishes. Some used in this book include:

Cinnamon Sweet spice commonly used for flavoring baked goods. The aromatic bark of a type of evergreen tree, it is sold as whole dried strips—cinnamon sticks— or ground.

Nutmeg Popular baking spice that is the hard pit of the fruit of the nutmeg tree. May be bought already ground or, for fresher flavor, whole, to be grated as needed.

Paprika Powdered spice derived from the dried paprika pepper. Available in sweet, mild and hot forms. Hungarian paprika is the best, but Spanish paprika, which is mild, may also be used.

Peppercorns Pepper, the most common savory spice, is best purchased as whole peppercorns, to be ground in a pepper mill or coarsely crushed as needed. Pungent black peppercorns are pepper berries picked slightly underripe and allowed to dry with hulls intact. Milder white peppercorns are fully ripened berries from which the hulls are removed before drying.

Red Pepper Flakes Coarsely ground flakes of dried red chilies, including seeds, which add medium-hot flavor to the foods they season.

Star Anise A small, hard, brown seedpod resembling an eight-pointed star, used whole or broken into individual points to lend its distinctive anise flavor to savory or sweet dishes. The spokes of the star contain small seeds.

Index

ACKNOWLEDGMENTS

The publishers would like to thank the following people for their generous
assistance and support in producing this book: Stephen W. Griswold, Sharon C. Lott,
Laurie Wertz, Ken DellaPenta, Tina Schmitz, and the buyers and store managers
for Pottery Barn and Williams-Sonoma stores.

The following kindly lent props for the photography: American Rag-Maison,
Biordi Art Imports, Candelier, Fillamento, Forrest Jones, RH Shop, Sue Fisher King,
Chuck Williams, Williams-Sonoma and Pottery Barn.